WHEN YOU DON'T HAVE THE WORDS

Praying the Psalms

"I have prayed the Psalms for over thirty years, and I have yet to read a book that more closely resonates with my experience than this one. If you want to know how the Psalms will reshape your prayers, sufferings, hopes, and beliefs about God, then this is the book for you."

—CHAD BIRD, 1517

"I can still remember the time—the exact day and hour—when I could no longer find any words to pray. In a season of profound disorientation as a pastor, the bottom completely fell out of prayer life. I will never forget how the Psalms leapt to life and gave me an incredibly rich and profoundly healing vocabulary for prayer. It saved my life. I have read a lot of works on the power of the Psalms in prayer, but this may be the most warm, honest, practical, and Christ-centered guide I have read. As a fellow struggler and all-too-often delinquent in prayer, I found Reed's invitation to Psalmic prayer to be generous and kind; his desire to help me draw near to Christ to be earnest and authentic; and his advice to be practical and wise. He made me feel like stumbling forward into a richer life of prayer was wholly possible because it is all by grace alone. There are chapters and exercises that surprised me in how they led me directly into communion with Christ. After all, the Psalms were the prayer book that sustained Jesus all the way to the cross. This will be the first book I will recommend to anyone who has felt like a failure in prayer and longs to encounter Jesus in every page of Scripture."

—ABE CHO, Redeemer City to City, New York

"Reed Dunn powerfully demonstrates the true purpose of the Psalms: not primarily to get our thoughts out, but to get Jesus's thoughts in. The psalms aren't merely tools for searching the soul; they are molds that shape us into the image-bearers we were made to be. If you are stuck in prayer—if your petitions are too shallow, your praises empty, your confession half-hearted—this book provides a radical and God-centered reorientation that will restructure the way you pray."

—THOMAS KEENE, Reformed Theological Seminary, Washington, DC

"This accessible book on praying the Psalms is packed with insight and wisdom and is bound to be of enormous help to readers intent on deepening their faith and their prayer life. I warmly commend it!"

—IAIN PROVAN, Regent College, Vancouver

"Reed Dunn provides a practical and theological guide for praying the entire Psalter. He addresses the challenges we face when praying the psalms of the righteous, imprecatory psalms, or pre-written prayers in general, and builds a strong argument for ways that this ancient practice leads Christians into deeper communion with God."

—RACHEL WELCHER, author of *Talking Back to Purity Culture*

WHEN YOU DON'T HAVE THE WORDS

Praying the Psalms

Reed S. Dunn

When You Don't Have the Words: Praying the Psalms

Copyright 2025 Reed S. Dunn

Lexham Press, 1313 Commercial St., Bellingham, WA 98225
LexhamPress.com

You may use brief quotations from this resource in presentations, articles, and books. For all other uses, please write Lexham Press for permission. Email us at permissions@lexhampress.com.

Unless otherwise noted, Scripture quotations are from the *ESV® Bible* (*The Holy Bible, English Standard Version®*), copyright © 2001 by Crossway Bibles, a publishing ministry of Good News Publishers. Used by permission. All rights reserved.

Print ISBN 9781683598060
Digital ISBN 9781683598077
Library of Congress Control Number 2024947109

Lexham Editorial: Rachel Joy Welcher, Jonathan Gardner, Katrina Smith
Cover Design: Sarah Brossow
Typesetting: Abigail Stocker

24 25 26 27 28 29 30 / US / 12 11 10 9 8 7 6 5 4 3 2 1

For my wife Lee Ann and daughters,
Jennalee, Adeline, and Tarikwa

Contents

A Prayer

O *Lord,* I am continually with you;
you hold my right hand.
You guide me with your counsel,
and afterward you will receive me to glory.
Whom have I in heaven but you?
And there is nothing on earth that I desire besides you.
My flesh and my heart may fail,
but you, O Lord, are the strength of my heart and
my portion forever.
For behold, those who are far from you shall perish;
you put an end to everyone who is unfaithful to you.
But for me it is good to be near you;
I have made the Lord God my refuge,
that I may tell of all your works.
Through Jesus Christ our Lord.
Amen.

Part 1

A Psalmic Orientation

Chapter 1

The Ancient Path

Thus says the L*ORD*: *"Stand by the roads, and look, and ask for the ancient paths, where the good way is; and walk in it, and find rest for your souls."*
Jeremiah 6:16

Throughout Scripture, we are encouraged to prioritize the presence of God. We are told to seek the Lord's presence continually and be constant in prayer (Psalm 105:4; Romans 12:12). The access we have to God is truly staggering. When we pray, our words mix and mingle with the chorus of creatures that surround the Lord's throne. Day and night those beings never cease to cry, "Holy, holy, holy, is the Lord God Almighty!" (Revelation 4:8). And our prayers are included among theirs. Our words rise like incense into a realm we can scarcely imagine (Isaiah 6:3; Psalm 141:2; Revelation 8:3–4).

The presence of God is a place of mystery and awe. It may be a place of dread for some, but for Christians, it is the source of our greatest comfort, joy, and security. We can speak directly to him whose very presence burned like fire in the wilderness. Yet we are welcomed in and nourished for being there. As Psalm 16:11 says, "In your presence there is fullness of joy; at your right hand are pleasures forevermore."

With such an encounter available to us, one would think Christians would rarely leave his presence, but it's more complicated than that. God's presence is marvelous, but it is also hidden. In the Old Testament, God shrouded himself in smoke or veiled himself within the temple. Because of Christ, those barriers have been removed, yet we find ourselves struggling all the same. Today, God veils himself in the ordinariness of life. When we meet God, we don't get to hear Sinai's trumpet blast or stand at the edge of the glassy sea. We simply pray; we take the sacraments; and we study God's word. God is no less present in these things, but they can feel surprisingly mundane.

Most of us would like a little more feedback, more assurance that what we see isn't all that there is. Twice in the book of Daniel, angels show up to assure him that his prayers were not only being heard, but they were being answered. First, Gabriel told Daniel that his prayers had been received and he was greatly loved (Daniel 9:23). Later, a second angel told him that a great spiritual struggle had delayed the response to his prayers (Daniel 10:12–13).

How nice if we had such assurance: to know that we were praying as we should, praying in the right direction even, and that God was responding. If angels appeared when I prayed, I'm sure I would pray more often than I do. But we rarely get that assurance.

Spirituality, for many of us, can feel like guesswork. We try what has worked for our friends and hope that it works for us. We might never even question whether our spirituality is the kind of spirituality that God wants for us.

We should have more clarity on something so important. If God wants us to seek him continually, surely he has offered us a way, some kind of template to guide our spiritual experience. We shouldn't have to figure it out for ourselves but, too often, that is what we do. We make our own path to God out of modern values and personal taste. We busy ourselves with missions because we like to measure our achievements. We bury ourselves in study because we prefer certainty over mystery. We exaggerate our joy in order to avoid the silence of God. None of these are necessarily bad, but something more certain is available.

God has provided a guide, an ancient path, that can lead us into his presence. This guide pierces through the veil of mystery with something that we can actually hold in our hands. It brings together the ordinary act of praying with divine words that come straight from God himself. It is true that God has hidden his presence, but he has also made himself available. We are not left to our imagination, and we are not expected to find our own way. We do not need to hack through some jungle or find our bearings in a trackless waste. Instead, we can simply follow our Lord wherever his ancient path leads.

God's ancient path is the path of psalmic prayer. It is a form of prayer that keeps us from wondering what we should say to God and how we should say it. Praying the Psalms takes much of the guesswork out of spirituality and tamps down our spiritual whims. Believers have been using psalmic prayer to meet God since the time of David and it works as well for us as it did for them. The Psalms are the original prayer book of God's people. In this book, we will explore what it means to pray them.

The Psalms as a Book of Prayer

When we read God's word, we observe those events that have already taken place. We even have to study things that would be obvious to the original audience because we are so far removed from what transpired. For instance, each plague in Egypt would have had particular significance to the people in that region, and the common Egyptian would have noticed it immediately. But we can only figure that out through study. We read Isaiah's prophecies and, to understand them well, we need to do significant background work on the politics of the ancient Near East. Even in the New Testament, we observe stories about Jesus and read letters written to ancient churches that are quite different from our own church experiences.

Scripture tells the stories of people who lived long ago, in far flung places. The Holy Spirit speaks to us through the word, so we are at no disadvantage, but we might feel like bystanders to an ancient conversation. When we do a Bible study, we snoop around those stories like detectives, trying to piece together significant details and highlight bits of information that will become important as the story unfolds. We need to study Scripture because we weren't there when it happened.

The Psalms, however, are different. They invite us into the middle of the story. They bring us into direct conversation with God. Simply reading a psalm turns us into the primary speaker and God into our audience. When Psalm 119:105 says, "Your word is a lamp to my feet and a light to my path," it is encouraging us to pray, not observe. We don't have to do a word search about feet or a background study about how ancient lamps were used. Instead, the psalm simply prompts us to tell God that his word is a lamp to our feet. It's that simple. We speak rather than observe. The words of that psalm become our words to God.

Athanasius argued this very point in the fourth century. He taught the church that the Psalms were given to us in a way that no other Scripture is:

> He who recites the psalms is uttering [them] as his own words,... as if they were written concerning him, and he accepts them and recites them not as if another were speaking, nor as if speaking about someone else. But he handles them as if he were speaking about himself. And the things spoken are such that he lifts them up to God as himself acting and speaking them from himself.[1]

Somewhere along the way, however, modern Christians started using the Psalms differently. We quit praying them and started seeing them as a record of someone else's experience. We study

Psalm 19 to learn about God's law. We read Psalm 63 to watch David in the cave. We read Psalm 137 and chuckle at Israel's wrath. Our penchant for examining Scripture may have become an obstacle to our using the Psalms. We inspect the Psalms as if they were happening inside a snow globe. We underline the inspiring bits, but mostly keep our distance from the experiences that they describe. And this robs us of the true purpose of the Psalter. The Psalms were meant to be *our* prayers and not just the words of ancient people.

The challenge, however, is greater than that. Modern Christians may be hesitant to pray the Psalms because we value our own words and experience over that of ancient people. We believe that prayers written by others cannot possibly be as heartfelt as our own. We assume that scripted prayers are rote, which we associate with thoughtless and inauthentic religion. We are living in one of the only times where believers have abandoned the practice of praying the Psalms, and I think that is because we prioritize the individual and the new over the community and the old.

Yet things are changing. Christians are beginning to embrace the past again. Some of us crave a weightier version of Christianity and long to feel connected to those who came before us. We want the creeds, the sacraments, and the liturgy. We want fathers and mothers in the faith. If you are reading this book on ancient prayer, then you probably already feel this in your bones. You are already aware that there is more to spiritual practice than the abridged spirituality that's offered by the contemporary church. As the modern church prioritized the self, it minimized the rest of Christian history. It rejected what seemed antiquated, only to discover that it was a source of depth and significance.

As I teach people to pray the Psalms, I love watching them realize that this is what prayer used to be like. They sometimes feel embarrassed, as if we were the first generation to forget how to use the wheel. And, in some sense, that's the case. We have made prayer much harder than it should be. We have put so much emphasis on praying in our own words that we have left people ill-equipped to find and experience the presence of God. And our fear of scripted prayers is unfounded. When the disciples asked Jesus how to pray, he didn't tell them to pray in their own words. Rather, he gave them a scripted prayer. He taught them a prayer that, as Dietrich Bonhoeffer noticed, seems to summarize the prayers in the Psalter.[2]

The Psalms are ancient prayers, used by ancient people, to meet the Ancient of Days. As we pray the Psalms, we have the chance to participate in that ancient conversation. We can speak words to God that he has been listening to for thousands of years. He crafted these prayers and, when we use them, our spiritual experience is shaped by his hand. The Psalms become the scaffolding for our Christian life, a scaffolding that God himself designed.

The Psalter and Its People

The book of Psalms has one hundred and fifty chapters, and each chapter is an individual prayer.[3] These prayers span the long life of Israel and range from every kind of spiritual experience. Psalm 90 is probably the oldest psalm, as it is attributed to Moses. Psalm 137, on the other hand, was written while Israel was in Babylon, a mere five hundred years before Christ. Almost half of the psalms were written by David, but others were composed by the leaders in temple worship (for example, Asaph and the Sons of Korah). Many of the famous prayers in the Old Testament are republished and repeated in various psalms. The Psalms also contain prayers from events that were recorded in Scripture (Psalm 51) and others that were not (Psalm 7).

These one hundred and fifty prayers were collected together by ancient editors. They selected the order, grouped them together, and occasionally included historical and musical notes in the way of introduction. We know almost nothing about these editors, but we assume that they were working under the direction of the Holy Spirit. One thing seems certain, these ancient editors wanted to provide the community of faith with a single place to go in order to find prayers to God. At the end of the second scroll of Psalms, one of the editors wrote, "This concludes the *prayers* of David, son of Jesse" (Psalm 72:20, emphasis added).[4] Those editors saw themselves as constructing a prayer book.

As a prayer book, the Psalter was a spiritual companion for the people of God. Psalms were recited during times of personal tragedy and national events. They accompanied offerings and gave voice in worship; they were recited during pilgrimages, festivals, and sabbaths. There were psalms that were used during coronations and even one for commemorating a king's wedding. Because they marked the highest and lowest moments, the Psalms offered a prayerful cadence to every aspect of life.

To us, however, the Psalms look more like poetry than prayer, and that can be misleading. You may have noticed this if you turned to the Psalms hoping to find some poetic ideal but instead found them talking about *Og, king of Bashan* (Psalm 135:11, 136:20). Many of the psalms seem completely uninterested in whether we are being inspired. Also, because the word *psalm* actually means *song*, it is tempting to think of the Psalter as a hymnal full of songs we will never sing. Poetry, however, had a different purpose for ancient people. They likely chanted the psalms instead of singing them, and the poetic structure made it easier to meditate on the words. Read a psalm out loud and you may notice the repetition. Phrases get repeated and often intensified, which gives the reader a chance to ponder a single idea in different ways.[5] Had the Psalter been nothing more than a hymnal, then the early church would have had no need to create their own "hymns and spiritual songs" (Ephesians 5:19).

These prayers were absolutely integral to the life of the ancient believer. In an age where we can curl up with the whole Bible, it's easy to forget that Scripture was largely unavailable to common people in the ancient world. Scripture was read in the synagogues and churches where it was kept. If a believer possessed any portion of the Bible, it was most likely a Psalter. For this reason, the Psalter acts as an abridged Bible that recounts history, teaches theology, and casts the hope and vision of the people. For those who didn't have a Psalter, the Psalms were recited so often that most scholars believe ordinary Jews would have had large portions of it memorized.

I find it marvelous that God wanted the Psalter to be the central text of religious life. God could have compiled a collection of laws, drawn from Exodus, Numbers, and Deuteronomy, but he chose to compile a book of prayers instead. That says something about who he is and what he wants from his people. He had so much he wanted to teach them, but he decided to teach them through recited prayer. He wanted prayer to be woven into their culture, to the point that psalms seemed to just roll off their tongue.

The triumphal entry of Jesus is a great example of this. During the Passover festival, the Jewish people prayed a collection of psalms called the Egyptian Hillel (Psalm 113–118). The words of those psalms would have been the backbone to that experience, ringing in the homes and synagogues as believers worshiped and gathered with old friends. On one such Passover, Jesus came into Jerusalem riding on a donkey. The people greeted him with the words they'd already been recited countless times, the words of the Egyptian Hillel: "Blessed is he who comes in the name of the LORD!" (Psalm 118:26 quoted in Matthew 21:9, Mark 11:9, and Luke 19:38)

The religious pilgrims probably chanted the whole psalm as Jesus entered the city, or at least large sections of it. In doing so, they proclaimed that the rejected stone was about to become the Cornerstone (118:22). They also cheered the fact that the Sacrifice was on its way to the altar (118:27). Unbeknownst to them, the crowd laid out the whole plan of the passion week. At that moment, however, only Jesus knew the significance of the words that the pilgrims were shouting in the streets.

Jesus embodied the hopes, theology, and practice that believers had learned through centuries of praying the Psalms. It's no wonder, then, that the first Christians expressed their new religion along the same psalmic lines. The Psalms figure prominently in the early church. The disciples used Psalms 69 and 109 as the basis for replacing Judas with Matthias (Acts 1:20). Peter, in the first Christian sermon, relied on Psalms 16 and 110 to prove the identity of the risen Lord. The first description of Christian worship includes a reference to believers reciting "*the* prayers," which was likely a mixture of the Jewish Shema and the Psalms (Acts 2:42, emphasis added). It's not surprising, then, that the first prayer recorded in the book of Acts began with a recitation of Psalm 2 (Acts 4:25–26).

With the coming of Jesus, everything changed. Food laws and circumcision were terminated and soon the temple followed suit. Jewish social order was transformed, as there was no longer a distinction between Jew, Greek, slave, free, male, or female (Galatians 3:28). It was a time of complete spiritual upheaval, yet psalmic spirituality stayed the same. The Psalms were as important in the church as they had been in the synagogue. The Psalter is quoted more than any other book by the New Testament authors, and the Psalms gave shape to everything from the crucifixion narrative to the book of Hebrews. Paul exhorted Christians to share psalms with each other, letting the word dwell in their hearts through the recitation of the Psalms (Ephesians 5:18–19; Colossians 3:16).

In the years after the apostles, the church began to further separate itself from Jewish identity. Christians created their own distinctives by replacing long-held Jewish practice. For example, in the first century, the Didache encouraged believers to pray the Lord's Prayer instead of the Jewish Shema and suggested new days to fast in order to differentiate themselves from Jews.[6] In the second century, Ignatius taught that Christians should no longer keep the Sabbath but "live in accordance with the Lord's Day."[7] Yet, as the Christian church built its identity and distinguished itself from Judaism, it didn't replace its practice of praying the Psalms.

The Psalter and Christian Spirituality

The spiritual practice that we explore in this book came into its own during the fourth century of the church. Believers may have used the Psalter the same way before this period, but we just don't know. Church history has largely focused its attention on leaders and heresies and rarely highlighted the practical spirituality of normal people. In the fourth century, however, things started to change. As Christianity became legal, believers could worry less about day-to-day survival. A new kind of Christian inquiry arose, one that popularized the soul's quest for God. And, as Christian spirituality became prominent, it's not surprising to see the Psalms at the center.

The Roman Empire legalized Christianity in AD 313 and, by 380, it was the state religion. This marked a sea change in Christian spirituality. Gone were the heroes who stood against civil magistrates. Gone was the persecution that purged the church of nominal believers. Christians even started to enjoy cultural and economic advantages over others as the Roman Empire experienced an ancient version of the "Bible Belt."

Reacting against a faith they saw as bloated, a small group of men and women in Alexandria, Egypt ventured into the Egyptian desert to prove their Christian mettle and meet their God. They considered themselves to be Christian athletes, enduring hardships that could no longer be found in the casual faith of the city. These people would become the first Christian monks. Whether we realize it or not, our modern experience of faith is deeply indebted to this community. They shined a spotlight on the inner life of the soul and inspired the world with their personal spirituality. It was then, for the first time, that Christians spoke and wrote openly about their personal connection with God.

These desert fathers headed into the wilderness with few worldly provisions and even less earthly direction. They sold their property and left their families. They essentially went into the desert blind, following rumors of hermits that had gone before them. They had little sense of the wilderness that stretched out before them, but the only path they cared to find was the path that led to God. This was a path they found mapped out in the Psalms. The Psalter formed the backbone of their spirituality. They prayed through the Psalter obsessively. There are stories of monks praying through the whole Psalter every day. They were extreme enthusiasts, to say the least, but their fanciful visions and outrageous experiences did not interrupt their ongoing commitment to praying the Psalms.

One of those spiritual adventurers was John Cassian. Like many educated young men with means, Cassian left it all to explore the deserts of Palestine and Egypt, living among the monks and learning their ways. He stayed in the desert for much of his life. Then, after years in the wilderness, he moved to southern France with the desert practices in tow. Cassian founded a monastery in AD 415, near the town of Marseilles and thus, western monasticism was born. In both the monastery and the church, psalmic prayer spread throughout Europe and became a mainstay for all those who prioritized spirituality. In 516, St. Benedict incorporated the practice of psalmic prayer into his *Rule*, and monks and nuns have been praying through the whole Psalter every week from then until now.

Prayers for Today

For most of its existence, the church has made use of the Psalter as a means of prayer. The list of famous Christians who encouraged the church to pray the Psalms is too long to recount in full. From Athanasius to Bonhoeffer, from Orthodox priests to Catholic nuns, and from John Calvin to Martin Luther; all of them used the Psalms as their own prayers to God. The first Christians prayed the Psalms as they huddled in the upper room and bishops in the

Church of England republished the Psalter when they created the *Book of Common Prayer*. From famous theologians to ordinary believers, Christians for two millennia have found psalmic prayer to be a primary path to God. Yet believers today hardly know that we can use the Psalter this way.

I hope that this book can help you rediscover this ancient practice. When I first started praying the Psalms, it was so easy that it felt like cheating. I couldn't believe that I could open up the Bible and have words there for me to use. Like most modern Christians, I had convinced myself that praying in my own words was the best way to pray, but I really had no good words to say to God. Praying the Psalms was, for me, like flipping on a switch. I suddenly knew how and what to say to God. I had spent years wishing I could pray instead of actually praying. I was weighed down by the guilt of it. The truth is that my prayer life needed help. It is that help that I want to share with you.

This book is divided into two parts. Part one is an orientation towards psalmic prayer. In the next chapter I will make my case that the Psalter is a key ingredient in our spiritual formation. Chapter 3 will consider some practical tips for praying the Psalms. Part 2 will focus on the experience of praying the Psalms. The goal there is to introduce aspects of the Psalter that are easily missed or hard to pray. It is not an exhaustive study. You may notice there is no chapter on confessing sin, because that is a straightforward topic both in psalmody and in life. At the end of each chapter there is a reflection. The point of these will be to practice what we've been learning. They will also give us a chance to consider some important topics that don't quite fit within the regular chapter.

The goal throughout this book is to make psalmic prayer, and spiritual practice in general, more accessible. Everyone has the right disposition to know and experience God, and interacting with him is easier than you might think. Eventually, praying them will become second nature, and I am confident that you will be blessed as you pray these ancient prayers. With practice, you will learn how to put your own hopes and fears into the words written by others. When that happens, you will begin praying prayers that God himself gave the church to pray. They are words composed in the presence of God, uniquely fitted for the presence of God.

This book is the fruit of my own spiritual journey. I don't pretend to be a Psalms scholar, but I do profess to be an avid Psalms pray-er. What I lack in credentials, church history has provided with countless fellow devotees. Martin Luther, for one, taught the church that the Psalter was a manual for prayer. He wrote,

> In my opinion, any man who will but make a trial in earnest of the Psalter and the Lord's Prayer will very soon bid the other pious prayers adieu, and say, Ah, they have not the sap, the strength, the heart, the fire, that I find in the Psalter; they are too cold, too hard, for my taste![8]

This has certainly been my experience. There simply aren't better ways to pray. There are reasons to pray in our own words, and history provides ample evidence of that practice, but God has made an ancient path that leads to his presence. He is inviting us to follow. So, as Jeremiah has encouraged us, let us stand by the road and ask about the ancient path. Let us walk that path together and find rest for our souls (Jeremiah 6:16).

Reflection 1: The Psalter King

Praying Psalms 20–24

This first reflection gives us the chance to consider the most important person to ever pray the Psalms. Jesus's life and ministry was saturated with the Psalter. He quoted the Psalms more than any other book during his ministry, and the writer of Hebrews pictured Jesus as a member of the holy congregation, singing psalms amidst his brothers and sisters (Hebrews 2:12).

Jesus became like us when he became a human being. He felt hunger and thirst, joy and pain. His life on earth was also marked by the spiritual experiences indicative of normal Christian life. Like us, Jesus lived by faith and talked to the Father through prayer. Just as it does for us, the Psalter articulated the trials and tribulations of his life in a fallen world. While the four gospels describe the facts of God's incarnation and Paul's letters detail its implications, the Psalms provide us with a window into Jesus's incarnation experience. Through those prayers, Christ's humanity unfolds. As he prayed the Psalms, he joined in our human experience. As we pray those same Psalms, we can reflect on his life among us.

The connections between Jesus's life and the Psalter are limitless. One connection, however, always seems to make an impression on me as I pray through the Psalter. It relates to his experience on the cross. One of his most famous sayings from the cross was, "Eli, Eli, lema sabachthani?" that is, "My God, my God, why have you forsaken me?" (Matthew 27:46, Psalm 22:1) Of all the things he said, this is the most heartbreaking, the most agonizing. It never fails to startle us.

Before I started praying the Psalms, I never thought of anyone, particularly Jesus, praying them. I assumed Jesus used that phrase from Psalm 22 like a quote instead of a scripted prayer. Of course, it voiced his anguish to the Father, which is technically prayer, but I never thought of Jesus actually praying through the Psalter in his quiet moments on the cross. Yet that is exactly what one scholar suggests.[9] Gordon Wenham noticed that Jesus quoted Psalm 22 at one point during the crucifixion and then, at a later point, Psalm 35. It led him to speculate that Jesus used the Psalter as a prayer book until his final breath.

In this first reflection, I would like to propose a spiritual exercise. I want to invite you to pray alongside Jesus with the words of the Psalms. In a later chapter, we will discuss how to pray the Psalms but for now, just read through them prayerfully. Become a prayerful observer of the emotional life of Christ. We've all heard sermons on the biology and physics of Roman crucifixion, with the goal of us understanding the physical price that Jesus paid. Through the Psalter, however, we can pray alongside him and wonder at his spiritual, rather than physical experience.

Let's begin with Psalm 20. It is a royal psalm and was probably used during the coronation of the king. It expresses the hope that things would go well for the one that God had anointed. Through Psalm 20, the people pray for God's blessing on the king. This was more than just wishing him well in his new job, because Israel's well-being depended on the king. God treated the people like he treated their king. The hope is that the king would be God's man. Psalm 20 requests that God keep the promises that he made to David (2 Samuel 7:14–15). It claims those promises in time and space.

> May [the LORD] send you [the king] help from the sanctuary
> and give you support from Zion!
> May he remember all your offerings
> and regard with favor your burnt sacrifices!
>
> May he grant you your heart's desire
> and fulfill all your plans! (vv. 2–4)

Then comes Psalm 21. If Psalm 20 proclaimed the hope, then Psalm 21 declared the reality. In this psalm, Israel praises God for keeping those promises. Psalm 21:2 rejoices, saying,

> You have given [the king] his heart's desire
> and have not withheld the request of his lips.

These were the prayers that Jesus might have prayed on the cross. He was the true king of Israel. If ever there was a king that God would help from his sanctuary, it would be Jesus. If ever there was a king that could have the desire of his heart, it was him. Yet the hope and the joy of these psalms fell flat. Jesus hung on a cross instead of riding out into battle. He was laughed at by others instead of being the most blessed forever. Far worse, the father-son relationship was being ripped apart, as the Father turned his back on his Son. The promise to David was that God would always be there and always stay faithful, no matter what. Psalms 20–21 were built on that promise, a promise that was in the process of being broken.

God the Father and God the Son had watched horrible kings do abominable things throughout Israel's history. Kings committed adultery, sought counsel from witches, sacrificed their children, and led Israel into idolatry. Throughout all those years, God still treated those kings as sons. God kept sending prophets to warn them and kept honoring their efforts of obedience. However, on the cross, the true King and the true Son heard only silence.

Psalm 22 is tragic at any level, but is even more so when following the hope and the joy of Psalms 20–21. "My God, my God, why have you forsaken me!" The heavens were shut to the one person for whom they should always be open. The first half of that psalm is a better description of the crucifixion than even the gospel writers provide. It was the ultimate defeat, the ultimate humiliation.

Then, however, Psalm 22 turns. The last third of the psalm dares to find hope in the midst of pain. I wonder if Jesus was able to follow the psalm. Was he able to think of all the "yet unborn" that would know him because "he had done it?" (v. 31) After praying through Psalm 22, did he find comfort in Psalm 23? Did it bring him the same peace that it has brought countless Christians who face tragedy? And then there's Psalm 24.

Psalm 24 was one of the first texts the early church used to show the resurrection and ascension of Christ. The doors of heaven, which were shut to him in Psalm 22, are now flung open in Psalm 24 and the exalted Son can walk right in. If Jesus prayed this psalm, did it fill his heart with hope? Did the heavenly splendor seem close at hand? The King of Glory would be going home soon.

I picture Jesus continuing to pray. He certainly lived out the holiness that is expressed in Psalm 26. When I pray that psalm, it encourages me to remain faithful. Did it do the same for him? Meanwhile, Jesus had used the imagery of Psalm 27 to describe his crucifixion, I wonder if he re-lived those prophecies as he prayed those words (Psalm 27:6; John 8:28, 12:32). By Psalm 31, his work on the cross was complete. Jesus could now thank the Father because, "you take me out of the net they have hidden for me" (v. 4) His death would be the ultimate foil to the evil that surrounded him. Then Jesus prayed a line from that psalm with his final few breaths: "Into your hand I commit my spirit."

In this chapter we have considered how the psalmic path is the ancient path. It was prayed by countless believers before us, but none are more important than Jesus. The ancient path is his path, for he is the Way, the Truth, and Life. He is the Word made flesh. In many ways, the Psalms are a kind of touchpoint between heaven and earth, where the interests of one meets the interests of others. But God incarnate is the ultimate. As part of his life on this earth he showed us how to go about the ancient path. The Psalms can only be our prayers because they were first the prayers of our faithful King. God is able to accept us because he rejected his Son. We never have to cry "My God My God! Why have you forsaken me?" because Jesus did.

I encourage you now to find communion with Christ in Psalms 20–24. Don't study them, as if to prove his existence or with the hope of teaching about his experience. No, simply meet him. Pray alongside Jesus in these psalms. Grieve with him in Psalm 22 as he saw the promises of Psalms 20–21 fail. Be comforted alongside him as Psalm 23 provides comfort. Hope with him as he must have sensed, through Psalm 24, the blessings on the horizon. We have so little of Jesus in our busy life, but praying his prayers is a way for us to experience communion with him. I invite you into that prayerful communion now.

Chapter 2

The Psalter as Spiritual Formation

The Psalter is a peculiar book because God intended us to actively use it. Instead of just observing the spiritual environment of the Psalms, we are drawn in. We participate in that environment as we pray through each psalm. When we read the apostle Paul, we learn theology. We read the Old Testament and the Gospels and watch the story unfold. Even the Proverbs stand over us, giving us advice as if they were the teacher and we, the pupil. But the Psalms invite us to do more than learn, watch, and obey. They invite us to participate in their anger and bubble alongside them in delight.

The question for us is whether we are willing to participate. At first glance, the Psalter can seem out of touch with modern, everyday experiences. There are no psalms about singleness or married life, about raising toddlers or giving up long-held dreams. And that's being kind. Plenty of them are so hot-blooded that they are hard to square with Christian principles. Three-quarters of them deal with conflict and that can wear thin. Most of us have enough conflict in life that we don't need it from our Bibles as well.

Yet the Psalter keeps beckoning. Each psalm is an invitation to have a particular spiritual experience with God. I must admit that for years I was reluctant to accept the Psalter's invitation. I didn't want to partake of its spiritual environment because I liked creating my own. But I did like the Psalms, at least a few of them, so I spent many years picking and choosing which ones I wanted to use. I never used the whole Psalter, I just had a small catalog of favorites. Like a conductor, I directed my own spiritual journey, and I included those psalms that pointed me in the direction I wanted to go.

At one point I only had about three that I regularly used. I read Psalm 63 when I was longing for God, Psalm 51 when I sinned against him, and Psalm 104 when I was hiking and found a pretty place to pray. Three psalms out of a hundred and fifty! As if picking up a hitchhiker, I would bring an occasional psalm onboard, but it had to be headed in the same direction as me and it couldn't get too rowdy along the way. I didn't know what to do with the other one hundred forty-seven. I could not incorporate the whole Psalter into my life because it would have meant going out of my way. It would mean entering a different spiritual environment, a psalmic one, and I was too busy constructing a spiritual environment of my own.

In this chapter, however, I would like to propose something completely different. I propose that we embrace the whole Psalter, and let it become the dominant influence in our spiritual experience.

I think that every psalm can and should be "our psalm." Included in that, I suggest that we quit choosing which psalms we use based on our spiritual tastes and the direction we want to go.

Scripture teaches that the self is not a dependable guide (Proverbs 20:24). We never know where God is taking us, and we hardly know what we need to get there. We can't even trust our best religious impulses. Therefore, Christians are always in the process of learning to trust themselves less and the things of God more. The Psalter is one of those things from God that we can trust. It is the perfect instrument to shape our spirituality and guide us to our Lord.

The Psalter's ability to shape our lives, however, comes from the Psalter as a whole. Psalmic prayer isn't about praying one psalm, it's praying all of them. If you have ever prayed a single psalm, you may have noticed this already. That one psalm might be helpful, but it probably was not transformative. Our prayer life fundamentally changes when we commit to praying each and every psalm. And that brings us to a fundamental assumption of this book: *praying all of the Psalms is as important as praying any of them.*

The Songs of Ascent as a Pilgrim Companion

I began to look at the Psalter differently when I spent a summer preaching through the Songs of Ascent (120–134). These fifteen psalms were used by the Jewish people when they made their annual pilgrimage to Jerusalem. They were supposed to travel to Jerusalem three times a year, and these psalms would have been their spiritual companion. Studying them changed my life and revolutionized how I saw the Psalter as a whole.

Jews were spread throughout the ancient world, and their pilgrimages were often quite long. They sometimes had weeks to meditate as they traveled. I picture the pilgrims praying the Songs of Ascent during the day and talking about them with fellow travelers at night. The anticipation of the festival—seeing old friends, swapping stories, relaying news, and keeping the religious rites—all of it would be woven together with the Songs of Ascent. These prayers would become an indistinguishable part of their expectations.

These psalms, however, are surprising. Only the first few of them have to do with people taking a long journey. Psalm 120 begins with a lament about living in foreign lands. From there, Psalm 121 prays for traveling mercies; Psalm 122 rejoices at arriving in Jerusalem; and Psalm 123 pictures the traveler in the presence of God. That's it. From there, the psalms go in all sorts of directions and are mostly unremarkable.

Paul described what it was like to travel in the ancient world, and it sounds incredibly dangerous (2 Corinthians 11:25–26). Because of that, I would expect the Songs of Ascent to have a few more psalms that ask for divine protection. I would also enjoy seeing some poetic symbolism. There could be a psalm about the wilderness wanderings and how that compares to the pilgrimage made by later believers. At the very least, I would love to see some psalms concentrate on the true purpose of the pilgrimage. These people were going to meet God, so I would expect to see some psalms delve into the mystery and power of that momentous event. Such psalms, however, do not exist.

The Songs of Ascent have little interest in describing what the people experienced as they traveled. What they do have, however, is an unexpected number of complaints—not about travel, but about other nations. The lament of Psalm 120 makes sense because it fits with the need to go to Jerusalem. But the complaints pick back up in the closing lines of Psalm 123: "Our soul has had more than enough of the scorn of those who are at ease" (v. 4). Psalm 124 opens with, "If it had not been the Lord who was on our side … when people rose up against us, then they would have swallowed us up alive" (vv. 1–3). These psalms were intended to direct people to the presence of God, so why do they encourage pilgrims to consider so much conflict and wickedness?

Most of us think that the Psalms are trying to describe our spiritual experience. The problem, of course, is that we usually don't know the real-world purpose behind each psalm, not unless the psalm itself states it. Many of the psalms come to us without historical context so we just guess what they describe, presuming to know how they should be used. But that's not the case for the Songs of Ascent. We know exactly what their purpose was: pilgrimage. Yet they don't describe the pilgrim experience. That makes me wonder whether we've been expecting the right thing from the Psalter all along. How are the Psalms supposed to function?

The Songs of Ascent don't try to describe the journey. Instead, God used these prayers to prepare them for the destination. He gave them prayers that would help them rehearse his truths before they ever set foot in Jerusalem. He wanted to condition them, to warm them to a certain perspective. He wanted to train them in what to think and how to act. In other words, the Songs of Ascent gave pilgrims the chance to practice the experience that God wanted them to have.

The Songs of Ascent as a Spiritual Map

The Songs of Ascent can be read like a spiritual map. They helped the pilgrim leave one world and embrace another. Physically speaking, to enter Jerusalem meant leaving places like Alexandria, Carthage, and Rome. Spiritually speaking, these pilgrims were being asked to leave the civic, commercial, and cultural domain of the gentiles. They weren't simply moving from one location to another; they were making a spiritual journey, trading one kingdom for another. In this, the Songs of Ascent were their guide.

Take, for instance, the complaints. After Psalm 124 declares that Israel was almost swallowed up alive, it rejoices that "we escaped like a bird" (v. 7) It pictures the wicked as predators with teeth, and the godly as those who escape solely because God is their help. According to Psalm 125, the safety from predators is found in the holy city. It is nestled between the mountains and safe from the assaults and rule of the wicked. Psalm 126 then pictures Israel as dried up from weeping, needing restoration from God. Psalms 127–128 read like proverbs, but Psalm 129 jumps right back into affliction. "The plowers plowed upon my back; they made long their furrows" (v. 3) That seems dark and combative for people on their way to a religious festival.

God, however, wanted to help these travelers let go of their worldly associations back home. Many of these Jewish pilgrims made a decent living among the gentiles. In fact, many of them were dispersed across the ancient world specifically for this fact. Even back when the exile was coming to an end, many Jews elected to stay in Babylon rather than scratch out a new life by returning to the promised land. By the time of the New Testament, life seems substantially better outside of Israel than inside of it. Across the Roman Empire, Jewish people were climbing important social ladders and gaining cultural and political influence. Herod the Great, after all, was friendly with Julias Caesar and Cleopatra!

Like any believer, the pilgrims might have found that the claims of their religion and their reality were in conflict with one another. Jerusalem is pictured as the most important city in the world, but the Alexandrian Jews were living in one of the greatest cultural centers to ever exist. The Bible speaks of Mount Zion as if it were the highest mountain in the world, but some pilgrims lived near snow-capped peaks in Cilicia. The temple, meanwhile, was portrayed as an eternal refuge that could never be shaken, yet some of these travelers were coming from Rome, known across the ancient world as the Eternal City.

What if the complaints in the Songs of Ascent weren't actually complaints at all? Instead of complaining, what if these psalms were training God's people, moving the pilgrim along a spiritual path that led them away from the refuge that this world provides? These pilgrims needed a change in perspective, and praying these psalms would do just that. Their perspective on wealth, security, and power would be reoriented towards a spiritual direction. In other words, what if God used these complaints to introduce doubt about worldly success and power? The Songs of Ascent would reframe the meaning of their day-to-day experience. Psalm 30 describes the situation quite well:

> I said in my prosperity,
> "I shall never be moved."
> By your favor, O Lord,
> you made my mountain stand strong;
> you hid your face;
> I was dismayed. (vv. 6–7)

The pilgrims who lived in the world's great cities and had enough money to travel needed to remember that the only immovable thing was God. They needed to remember that he was the giver of life. And what better way to do this than to pray prayers of affliction? Through these prayers, the pilgrims were reminded of the longstanding enmity between the seed of the woman and the seed of the serpent. They were shaped by these prayers, prayers that directed their feet, as well as their hearts, to the true Eternal City.

Of course, some of these pilgrims did experience affliction, but *all* of the pilgrims were supposed to pray *all* of these psalms.

They weren't supposed to pick and choose which psalm fit their circumstances. Rather they were being asked to rehearse all of the truths contained within the fifteen Songs of Ascent. In doing so, they would be prepared for the festival event and, by the time they entered Jerusalem, the blessings of Zion would far outstrip the blessings they might find in Alexandria, Carthage, or Rome. And it was the psalms that got them there. The psalms didn't fit the people, the psalms fit the people for God.

The Psalter and Muscle Memory

This was a revelation for me. It shows me why my previous way of using the Psalms was shallow, and why it left me feeling empty. As modern Christians, we assume that our experiences and knowledge are the bedrock from which we build our spirituality. If we find a psalm useful, it's because it matches our experience or teaches us something that we want to learn. We begin with the self, with our preferences and our journey. When it comes to spirituality, we are too often the sculptor *and* the clay.

Here, though, is a different way to think of it. In psalmic prayer, we pray all of the Psalms and discover God's preferences and conform to his journey. Instead of looking for just the right psalm to describe how we feel, psalmic prayer pushes us to pray all kinds of psalms regardless of our feelings. The Songs of Ascent show us that the self does not have to be the bedrock of our spiritual experience, that there is something better. The Psalms can prescribe our spirituality and not just describe it. They can form us into a spiritual size and shape that God, himself, has chosen. The Psalms shape us through practice.

When I was learning to play golf, I had an instructor who made me practice every detail of the golf swing. I was a middle-school kid who really just wanted to drive a golf cart, but he had me swing a club so slowly that, at every point in the swing, I could tell if I was in the proper position. Were my hands rotating, weight shifting, and elbow tucking? We practiced this over and over. Nowadays, I hardly ever play golf but, when I do, friends are surprised at my swing. What I practiced slowly (and repeatedly) has been seared into my brain, such that a pretty golf swing comes naturally to me. All that practice created muscle memory.

My golf instructor knew what my middle-school self did not: there are so many things that happen in a golf swing that you can't possibly keep it straight at full speed. And if that's true of golf, how much more is it true of life? Even now, as someone dedicated to praying the Psalms, I find that "just the right psalm" doesn't always help me when I need it. Sometimes things are happening too fast or problems are too large, and I have nothing but the reflexes I have built up over time. At such moments, psalmic prayer is more helpful than ever.

This is never clearer than when I am having a particularly difficult season in life. There are times we face problems too large for us, like changes at work or problems at home. Financial struggles are always a trigger for me. They cause instant panic. In the midst of my little meltdowns, there have been very few times that I have turned to something like Psalm 64 and, in that moment, found all the comfort that I need. I love the passage from Matthew 6 about God clothing the fields and feeding the birds, but when I am wrestling with fear, it doesn't always move the needle of my heart as much as I want.

Similarly, the psalms about God's provision are at their most helpful when we pray them in the weeks and months leading up to a crisis of faith. Praying only in the moment is like trying to learn how to drive a tank in the middle of a war. It's too late by then. We have to learn how to believe before the alarm bells ring. Conversely, praying about God's providence before we need to trust in it prepares us for those moments when our trust is shaken. The Psalms do their best work before the bullets ever start flying.

Much like those pilgrims were prepared for the festival by the Songs of Ascent, we are prepared for our present trials by the prayers that we have prayed in the past. The faith we need to combat our fear must be summoned long before we are surrounded by the fears and troubles of the moment. The psalms help us create spiritual reflexes that can respond to crises far better than troubleshooting in the moment.

That is the muscle memory that psalmic prayer can provide. When we pray through all of the Psalms, we inevitably pray things that seem irrelevant at the time, but that is the point. The best preparation happens when we have to prayerfully contort ourselves into the shape of something different. In psalmic prayer, nice people have to curse; faithful people have to doubt; angry people have to wait; and controlling people have to trust. Praying through all the Psalms requires that we practice all of those positions.

Within the scholarly community, there are debates about how many types of psalms there are in the Bible, whether five or seven. When it comes to psalmic prayer, I would say there are one hundred and fifty types. Each psalm provides us the opportunity to work new spiritual muscles. They show us how to grieve before tragedy strikes and how to rejoice when there's nothing to celebrate. They aren't just describing how we feel, they are preparing us to feel. Even the psalms that quote other psalms use the same information in different ways, juxtaposing the same content against different backgrounds.

The Psalter and Spiritual Stability

There is a remarkable section in Psalm 32 that gives us a wonderful picture of Christian maturity. God speaks to the psalmist:

> I will instruct you and teach you in the way you should go;
> I will counsel you with my eye upon you.
> Be not like a horse or a mule, without understanding,
> which must be curbed with bit and bridle,
> or it will not stay near you. (vv. 8–9)

I don't know about you, but it sometimes feels like I can only stay close to God if he has me on a short leash. When I head in my own direction, God is quick to respond. His response is always loving, but not always pleasant. "When you discipline a man," says one psalm, "you consume like a moth what is dear to him" (Psalm 39:11). Another says to God, "Let the bones that you have broken rejoice!" (Psalm 51:8). Yet another says, "It is good for me that I was afflicted, that I might learn your statutes" (Psalm 119:71). In other words ... *ouch*! What we learn in times like this is that God can be as tough as our hearts.

For immature Christians, God seems to not have our full attention unless we are being humbled, in pain, or we are broken. In those moments, it may feel as though God has burned all the bridges we make for ourselves, just so we will walk over the right one. This is the bit and bridle of Psalm 32. I used to think that was the only way I could grow as a Christian, when circumstances left me with no other choice. But Psalm 32 also tells us that it doesn't have to be that way. God doesn't like the bit and bridle any more than we do. There is a way of relating to him where we are in tune with his will and respond without force. We can stay near to him because he has directed our steps with his counsel. This is the gold standard of Christian obedience. It is life in the Spirit.

Psalmic prayer offers believers the opportunity to practice living in the Spirit. I like to think that the Psalms provide us the chance to learn the table manners we need as we feast with our Lord. They also give us the chance to rehearse our fight against the flesh, which so often gets in the way. Through practicing spirituality, we can anticipate sin and learn its favorite moves. We become more sensitive to sin's enticement and more hardened in standing against it. The result is that we get less bit and bridle and more gentle leading. In psalmic prayer, I have found something that I have searched for in every corner of Christian spirituality: spiritual stability. Since praying the Psalms, I have fought with God less, believed him more, and walked alongside him better.

The reason for this is that I'm now regularly praying through things that used to derail me. As we pray the Psalms, we must express faith in God even when we don't have it; we learn to doubt him without scoffing; and we pray our way through sin and learn how to confess. Psalmic prayer doesn't fix our sin problem, but it does help us identify it quicker and respond to it better. It doesn't keep us from life in a fallen world, but it does strengthen our defenses against it. In short, praying all of the Psalms offers us the opportunity to become skilled at the Christian life.

Psalm 1 introduces the whole book by using the imagery of a tree planted by a stream of water. Such a tree is always nourished, and it grows strong in the environment hand-crafted by the Lord. It has what it needs and, therefore, it produces as it should. There is no need for extra rain, no fear of the heat, and no need to be anxious in times of drought (Jeremiah 17:8). For the believer, this tree represents a spiritual life without all the drama. There is no dark night of the soul for such a person, for they know the source and continually draw from it. It is the picture of stability.

Psalm 1 is a peaceful scene, even though the wicked are nearby. Much like Psalm 23, the peace of Psalm 1 is a peace in the presence of enemies, which is the only kind of peace we can have this side of glory. The scene is peaceful because the wicked have no influence. The righteous have been fortified from the inside by the nutrients of God. Another psalm describes the righteous as unafraid, firm, trusting, and steady (Psalm 112:6–7). This is the kind of life the Lord wants for his children. It's the peace that surpasses all understanding, and a kind of peace that the world cannot give.

The tree of Psalm 1 is at the beginning of the Psalter for a reason. It is the principal image of the whole book. The Psalter is that stream that nourishes the soul. However, this nourishment is not complete if we pick and choose which parts we use. Neither will we find this peace if we wait for it to come naturally. Salvation is a gift from God, but we can't simply live out that salvation through our own spiritual talent. Life in the Spirit is progressive and is subject to our cooperation and improvement (2 Corinthians 3:18).[10] That improvement only comes through maturity; maturity only comes through growth; growth only comes through practice, which can best be accomplished through prayer.

Let us, then, step on that ancient path and make our pilgrimage to God. As we do, let us be shaped by the hand of God as we enter the spiritual environment of the Psalter and we let go of whatever it is that we constructed for ourselves. Let us experience God the way he wants us to, building muscle memory for the long journey ahead. Let the whole Psalter be your guide.

Reflection 2: On Worship

Praying Psalm 96

In this chapter, we have examined the idea that praying the entire Psalter shapes our spirituality in ways we might not otherwise experience. Psalmic prayer may surprise you. You may find that you start praying prayers that you have long neglected and that you pray old favorites less often.

One surprise for me was how much less I prayed for others when I started praying through the Psalter. It took me a while to sort this out. Eventually, I realized I could pray the Psalms on behalf of fellow believers, but I was still struck by how much less intercession there is in the Psalter than there was in my prayer life.[11] Before I started praying the Psalms, I hardly prayed anything other than prayers of intercession. The length of my prayer time was directly tied to how many people I had to pray for. It wasn't because I loved people all that much, but more because I didn't know what else to say to God.

Praying the Psalms, however, directed me towards some long-neglected forms of prayer, and I no longer needed a list of people in front of me in order to spend time with the Lord. Of course, intercessory prayer is a sacred practice and a necessary part of the Christian life, but if it doesn't dominate the Psalter then maybe it shouldn't dominate our meeting with God. One thing that does dominate the prayers in the Bible is worship, and worship was probably the thing I did least. When I was praying in my own words, I narrowed the scope of what prayer could be and I cut out a fundamental aspect of why we pray in the first place. Psalmic prayer forced me to worship.

We don't worship enough. Few of us have been taught how to simply sit at the Lord's feet and admire him. We don't know what to think, what to say, or what we are supposed to do. Back in the days when I wanted to be a mystic, I remember setting aside the time and preparing myself with severe fasts, and then, when it came time to contemplate God, there was an overwhelming sense of "now what?" I had no idea how to actually meet him. Even our theology books are filled with things other than the person and the presence of God. I find this troubling.

If we think of spirituality in terms of concentric circles, the closer someone is to the presence of God, the more worship is their primary experience. Four creatures around the throne of God are the closest beings to him and, consequently, they do nothing but praise him day and night. They don't intercede and they don't go share the gospel. Every aspect of their being is swallowed up in the glory of God. I always wonder if they even know that we humans exist! They were created to glorify God, but we were made to do the same. Our methods differ from theirs, of course, but the existence of those four creatures stands as a challenge to our prayerful self-absorption.

The Psalms, however, can redirect us. They worship God at every turn.

I went on a spiritual retreat soon after I started praying the Psalms, and it was the opposite of my mystic wannabe days. I didn't have to fast or arrange meaningless details. Instead, I could sit before the Lord for an extended period of time and worship at his footstool using the words of the Psalter. The Psalms praise God as they recount history and prepare for battle; they praise him when they cry in agony and when they dance in the street.

Psalms 92–100 are the greatest hits of psalmic worship. To pray through this string of psalms is to join those four creatures surrounding God's throne. The 140s, meanwhile, have a more progressive approach. They begin with conflict and turmoil, but the theological vision slowly rises until they erupt with Psalm 150, where everything that has breath praises the Lord.

As you let go of your own spiritual environment and are shaped by psalmic prayer, worship will become more central to your spirituality. The Psalms will show you how. They will draw you along with their words as they give God the adoration that he deserves. However, psalmic prayer will do more than provide words. They also challenge our deepest misconceptions about worship. The Psalms will dislodge our long-held belief that worship is an emotional encounter with God.

The Psalms are not trying to describe our experience or put words to how we feel; we have seen that throughout this chapter. The Psalms are getting us to pray all kinds of things regardless of how we feel. And worship is just a part of that. There will be times that you will worship God simply for the fact that the psalm that you are praying is a psalm of worship. You aren't *feeling* it, you are *praying* it. This, for many of us, is a revolutionary idea.

Most of us think of worship as fundamentally emotional. Our feelings drive our worship. In fact, we call it hypocritical to worship when we struggle to keep our heart in it. As if we can only worship God when we are oozing worshipful emotions. We have to be overflowing with gratitude and awe. We picture earnest Christians looking heavenward, tears streaming down their cheeks, as if that was authentic worship. If you love to look heavenward and weep, then please don't let this stop you. But a lot of us don't feel that way; maybe never. What are we supposed to do?

Praying all of the Psalms requires that we drop such silly expectations. I regularly find myself in the great psalms of praise without the least bit of emotion to draw from. I praise God because those psalms are next in line, not because they necessarily describe how I feel at that moment. Psalmic prayer has taught me that my emotions are not the source of worship. God's worthiness is.

Psalm 96:8 has a short phrase that helped me understand worship as much as anything ever has. It says, "Ascribe to the LORD the glory due his name." That is what it means to worship, to ascribe the value of God to God. It's a verbal (and spiritual) transaction where we give God something that we owe him. Our job as created, dependent creatures is to offer the things to God that are due him. If we do that, then we have done our job.

Think of the implications of this. Emotions aren't part of it. We don't have to be giddy about God to ascribe value to him. We certainly shouldn't withhold our praise until we have an outpouring of emotions. He is owed worship, so we give it. Every month, we owe money to the electric company and we pay it. We don't wait until we are overcome with thankfulness for our lights, and we don't have to send a long-winded note with our bill. We owe them and we pay them. Similarly, God is due praise and glory, so we give it to him through worship. We don't have to feel it in order to do it.

It's that easy. Worship means telling God what is true. As part of my prayer time, I usually recite Revelation 4:11 that says, "Worthy are you, our Lord and God, to receive glory and honor and power." I mean those words when I say them, but I don't have to squeeze out some constipated emotions. Of course, there are times that I do feel it. There are times that my emotions catch up to my worship and I am overwhelmed by the glory and majesty of God. That's always pleasant, but it's no more real. Worship happens because of who God is, not because of how we're feeling.

We can worship God without having to whip ourselves into frothy gratitude. More to the point, we can worship him even when there is no gratitude to be frothed. Some readers may find this freeing, while others may be alarmed. Some Christians are suspicious of Christian activity whose source is not emotional. Some say that we aren't being genuine unless we are filled with gratitude for salvation or yearning for his presence. They might see this as a thinly veiled form of legalism. But I would remind those readers that we are in a long-term relationship with the Lord and it will ebb and flow with everyday life. Our primary calling is to worship God and that can't only happen at the behest of something as unreliable and self-centered as human emotions.

Psalmic prayer does not ask how you feel and then match your mood with prayer. On the contrary, it is a regimen of prayer that sometimes overlooks your mood in order to form you into the image of Christ. If you are anything like me, your lack of feeling has always carried with it a secret guilt. None of us could possibly feel thankful or giddy enough about salvation. But we don't have to. We worship God because of what is true of him, not us. We worship him when his divinely inspired prayers direct us to, not just when we feel like it.

With all of that being said, it is now time to worship God. I suggest using Psalm 96. The goal of this exercise is to praise God without having to feel it. As you pray, you should mean the words, directing them to God, but there is no need to feel any particular emotion. This prayer, after all, is about God, not you. Sometimes we can use our religious experience to subtly put ourselves on center stage, or we pursue an experience instead of the Lord. As you worship God through this psalm, don't wiggle your way into the middle of it. In the words of John the Baptist, let him increase and you decrease. Be a created being that ascribes to God the worth of his glory. Do it out of obedience with no regard for your emotions.

After you pray Psalm 96, shut your Bible and know for certain that you just worshiped God.

Chapter 3

How to Pray the Psalms

Praying the Psalms can be a lifelong pursuit. There are few spiritual practices as rich and nourishing. Over the years, I've taught many people how to pray the Psalms and I have witnessed its transformative effect. I have seen fellow believers pray the Psalms in the face of life's greatest tragedies and watched as the Psalms helped them find their voice in the presence of God. I am excited to share this practice with you and in this chapter, we will learn how to do it. This will be a practical examination of the most helpful techniques that I have discovered and used as I have prayed the Psalms over the years.

Praying the Psalms is as simple as it sounds. We use the words of the Psalms as our own words to God. It sounds easy, but there is sometimes a learning curve. The Psalms are chock-full of pronouns and language that can make direct speech to God a little cumbersome. The Psalms are also brimming with people we don't know and places we've never visited. Praying these prayers will require that we process David's pain and betrayal as if it were our own. That, of course, just scratches the surface. Praying the Psalms will eventually lead us to accuse God of outright neglect and pat ourselves on the back. Hardly anyone would pray like this if they weren't being directed to by Scripture. In Part 2 of this book, we will investigate the trickier parts of the Psalter, but first, we simply need to learn how to make the Psalms our own.

Speaking to God

When we read the Bible, it is easy to occasionally tune out. I've read 1 Samuel more times than I can count, but it wasn't until I was going to preach on it that I noticed the part where Michal makes a fake David with a pillow and some goat hair. Those are my favorite kinds of stories in the Bible, and I can't believe I'd ever missed it. Stories and truths sometimes sneak past without our noticing. When we use the Psalms as a prayer book, the same thing can happen. Prayer is difficult as it is, and reading prayers that were written by others can add to the challenge.

There is a reason that the ancient monks spoke of attentiveness in prayer as often as they talked about prayer itself. Meeting God is difficult. Attentiveness, for me, means taking time to focus on the person of God. Those monks recommended that we begin our prayer with a time of quiet meditation. If only for a moment, this stillness can settle our minds and direct our hearts. If ancient monks living in the middle of the desert struggled to focus on God, how much more will we? Realistically, there will be times when we can't ever get focused, or we pray just to check it off our list of things to do. That struggle is part of the process and it's okay, but taking a few moments to simply be in God's presence will help.

Another practice that will help you pray the Psalms is learning how to mean the words as you pray them. The enemy of prayer is detachment. Every Sunday before church, we do a microphone check where I distractedly count off some numbers. The words have no meaning. Things were quite different, however, when my daughters were learning their numbers. Back then, those same numbers had immense meaning. They were the same numbers, but my reason for saying them changed. I squeezed love into those little words, coaxing my daughters' response. The numbers one, two, and three were not addressing my children, but I was. If we can love our children while reciting numbers, then we can love the Lord while reciting the Psalms.

Prayer is the very bedrock of Christian spirituality because it is a direct conversation between two personal beings. We can experience God in other ways—like service and study—but in those disciplines, our interaction with him is mediated by what we are doing or what we are learning. Prayer is unique because it is so personal. It is an unobstructed, un-mediated interaction with the Lord. As one spiritual writer put it,

> When we pray to God, we're actually talking to him just as we talk to one another. God is our Father. We have no relative or friend here on earth who understands us and loves us as the Lord does.[12]

When you pray, cultivate your awareness of this loving and well-known person. His presence surrounds you even when you don't feel it. Think of him, direct your words to him, and meet him. God is there, in his word, and when we put our hearts into those same words, we meet him person-to-person.

How to Pray the Psalms

I've found that there are basically three ways to pray the Psalms. I'm calling them "methods" for the sake of ease, but that makes it sound more technical than it is. These methods describe the various relationships between the words of the psalm and the words that we pray. Each method offers a tighter or looser connection to the psalm, which results in different advantages and disadvantages. We will consider each method and what it offers the believer. I will give examples and be as practical as possible. However, I will not be discussing more meditative practices like memorization or *lectio divina*. Those techniques may be useful but belong in a different book. This book is about everyday prayer and how to incorporate the Psalter into it.

Method One: The Personal Approach

The first method is probably the easiest, at least at the beginning. Psalmic prayer is unique because, by praying the Psalms, we let go of our own prayer life. We pray what God wants us to pray, following the path that he has laid. At the same time, we are expected to stay engaged as we pray, pouring out our hearts before the Lord. This first method offers a nice balance: it's personal enough that we can express ourselves, but it keeps to the script enough that we are able to go where the Psalms take us.

In this method, we mostly read the words as they appear on the page, but we occasionally change some words to make them easier or more personal to pray. It always surprises me how much more personal a prayer feels if I interject the occasional "Lord" or "God." Secondly, in this method we might change the pronouns so as to make it direct speech. There is a lot of third person language in the Psalms, and you either have to get used to it or change it (see below). Lastly, this method offers the freedom to occasionally go off script for a moment and speak to God about a related matter or your own reflections.

Here is an example of this method from Psalm 107:17–22. Notice how praying the psalm causes me to enter the existential space of the psalm. This isn't a case of reading it and thinking about it, nor is it a case of watching some hapless bloke struggle with some unnamed problem. No, this is prayer, and when I pray the words, it becomes *my* prayer.

The psalm says:

> Some were fools through their sinful ways,
>   and because of their iniquities suffered affliction;
> they loathed any kind of food,
>   and they drew near to the gates of death.

> Then they cried to the Lord in their trouble,
>   and he delivered them from their distress.
> He sent out his word and healed them,
>   and delivered them from their destruction.
> Let them thank the Lord for his steadfast love,
>   for his wondrous works to the children of man!
> And let them offer sacrifices of thanksgiving,
>   and tell of his deeds in songs of joy!

We might pray:

> God, I've been a fool because of my sinful ways.
>   And because of my iniquity I've suffered affliction
>   (*maybe I add a specific example if I'm in the midst of one*).
> I loathed to eat any kind of food and because of it,
>   I drew near to the gates of death.
> Then I cried to you Lord in my trouble,
>   and you delivered me from distress.
> You sent out your word.
>   You've healed me!
>   You've delivered me from destruction.
> Thank you Lord for your steadfast love;
>   your wonderful works towards me.
> And Lord, I will offer sacrifices of thanksgiving to you
>   and I will tell of your deeds.
> You've put a song in my heart.

A note of caution is in order. Inserting our own words will inevitably provide a temptation to soften the psalm. We don't have the right to do that. Neither should we ever stand outside of a psalm and wish that the things in the psalm were true. We will cover this elsewhere, but as you try this yourself, you should start with good habits. The key to praying the Psalms is praying the words that are in the Psalms. If that sounds easy to do, then you've not yet prayed a hard psalm.

Along with that temptation there are a couple of disadvantages to this method. First, switching the pronouns can get confusing. The point of prayer is to speak to God, not get bogged down in middle-school grammar. Once, when I was still new to psalmic prayer, I prayed for someone in my church using Psalm 91. They were very ill and it's the perfect prayer for that occasion, but I should have given it a once-over before jumping in. Psalm 91 starts out well and is straightforward. At some point, however, things change. God starts speaking to the person that is writing the psalm about the person that is in need of the psalm. I got so confused by what all was going on that I had to stop praying, apologize, and restart the whole thing. The family needed a reason to laugh, but I didn't expect my psalmic prayer to be the cause.

My flub highlights the disadvantage of this method. It can be slow and it can make your prayers complicated. Also, there is a lot in the Psalter that is simply hard to cajole into a personal prayer.

What do you do with God casting his shoe on Edom or the envy that Mt. Bashan has for Mt. Zion? All this transposing and interpretation makes it an arduous way to pray. I like to pray through the Psalter more quickly, experiencing it in broad brushstrokes. This more meditative approach bogs me down into the details which can be good but also a bit boggy.

Disadvantages aside, there isn't a more intimate form of psalmic prayer. Anytime I'm praying with or for someone, I use this method. It just makes for a heartfelt time of prayer. I also use this method when I'm in a time of personal need. Changing and adding words forces us to slow down and wrestle with God in prayer, and we need that when we feel distant from him. It forces us to engage. For all those same reasons though, this method can be a bit draining.

Method Two: The Literal Approach

This method is straightforward enough, simply pray the Psalms exactly as they are written. If you like the simplicity of opening your Bible and having the prayer laid out before you, then this method is for you. It also appeals to people who like the fluidity of the Psalter. Prayed briskly, the repetition of the Psalms can act like a drumbeat in prayer.

Consider Psalm 107:17–22 again:

> Some were fools through their sinful ways,
>   and because of their iniquities suffered affliction;

they loathed any kind of food,
    and they drew near to the gates of death.
Then they cried to the Lord in their trouble, and he
  delivered
    them from their distress.
He sent out his word and healed them,
    and delivered them from their destruction.
Let them thank the Lord for his steadfast love, for his
    wondrous works to the children of man!
And let them offer sacrifices of thanksgiving, and tell of his
    deeds in songs of joy.

Here's the challenge of this method: does it feel like prayer when you speak of other people's predicament and how God, in the third person, delivered them? Our goal is to make these prayers our own. Intimacy with God is fundamental. Some believers may find nothing but distance when they pray the words exactly as they are written, and certainly that can be a challenge. I've struggled with this too. There have been plenty of times that I was using this method for a while, only to realize that I had actually quit praying some time ago. When I realize that I've disengaged, I usually go back to the first method until I get my prayer legs back under me.

However, it is definitely possible to pray like this. Thinking back to when I taught my daughters to count, I know we can give deep meaning to almost anything we say. We can read about these foreign people and distant lands and still speak to the

God we love. Some people may find it a bit isolating to pray about such distant things, but I actually have found the opposite. When I pray the Psalms exactly as they are written, I join the ancient people. I'm going through their trials and being delivered alongside them. I become a prayerful participant in a larger story.

This is a major purpose of the Psalms. They bring us into fellowship with God's people through prayer. Consider the great historical psalms, like Psalm 78, 105, and 106: God wanted his people to prayerfully recount the sacred history. He wanted them to identify with the wilderness generation even though the wilderness was long past. Individualists that we are, we want to pray about ourselves, but God arranged it so that his people would process the experience of past generations. To put it plainly, praying psalms about distant lands and people is not a shortcoming of psalmic prayer; it is prayer as God designed it to be.

This highlights something I have come to love about this second, more literal method. Over the years of praying with both methods, I have noticed that in the first method the Psalms belong to me, but in the second method I belong to the Psalms. It is a difference that is hard to explain but easy to feel. With this second method I can laugh alongside Israel as she taunts the Jordan River, "What ails you, O sea, that you flee? O Jordan, that you turn back?" (Psalm 114:5) With the first method I might be tempted to find a personal equivalent, subtly making the psalm about myself and my circumstances. In the second method I get sucked into the revelry, even when it has nothing to do with me.

Another benefit of this method is that it's the oldest form of psalmic prayer. Praying the Psalms as they were written means adding your voice to the long list of believers who used this script in ages past. These are the words that David and Asaph prayed as they wrote. These are the words that guided John's worship on the Isle of Patmos, and the same that Paul recited as he traveled the known world. Translations aside, these are the exact words that were chanted in synagogues and filled the very first house churches. These words, as they are written, are the words of our God.

Finally, this method is more flexible. Some of you may find that you can pray better when you listen. I love to listen to the Psalter being read. I can follow them in prayer as they lead me into the presence of the Lord. You may also want to try your hand at chanting. That is the oldest way to pray the Psalms and some people find it pulls them deeper into the prayer experience. Catholic and Orthodox traditions have different styles of chanting, which can make for a fun deep dive on the internet.

As you put these methods into practice, you may decide that one feels more natural to you than the other. You should pray in whatever way that feels natural, but don't be afraid to experiment. I've discovered that I love to pray the Psalms out loud, as fast as I can possibly read. When I do that, the intensity of my prayer soars. I never would have known that had I assumed I was supposed to quietly meditate. When I tire of that, I slow down and chew on every word. Try chanting, try listening, try speaking aloud, try meditating slowly, and try praying as fast as you can. Find a style of prayer that you like and switch when it gets boring. All of it is prayer if you speak the words to God. There is no rush to find a favorite and no need to stick with one thing. These one hundred and fifty prayers are the prayers you can pray for the rest of your life. You have all the time you need to explore.

Method Three: The Reflective Approach

In this final method, we use the Psalms as a kind of outline. We read a verse or phrase, and then reflect on it with our own short prayer. It may sound similar to the first method but it's quite different. In the first method, you change the occasional word to make the psalm more personal. In this third method, you read a psalm as is, but then echo it with your own prayerful response.

As far as personal prayer is concerned, I find this to be the lesser of the three methods. A major reason that I pray the Psalms is to get less "me" in my prayers. This method can have a whole lot of us in it. This method doesn't push us to conform to the Psalter as we typically reflect with our own thoughts and tastes. Conforming to the Psalter, for me, is the whole reason to pray the Psalms, so any method that does less than that is less appealing to me.

Disadvantages aside, this method is wonderfully helpful in particular situations. The call and response style of this third method makes it ideal to pray in groups. This can be a powerful experience.

One person reads a verse and every member of the group echoes the reading with a short prayer of their own. I love doing this with people. I often prefer it over Bible study. There is no need to do background studies, no need to have a clear leader, and no need to hear people go on and on about what they know. Just grab some friends and a psalm and meet God together. We don't do that often enough.

This is also a fun way to pray with kids. Anyone who struggles with family prayer time might find this a short and welcome practice. I'm always struck by how simple and honest the words of the Psalms are. Our kids need to see that. They need to see that God understands their experience. The psalmist speaks of having friends whose "words were softer than oil, yet they were drawn swords" (Psalm 55:21) Every middle-school child has to deal with that every day when they go to school, sometimes more often than adults. The Psalms can help them pray through that experience.

Here is an example from Psalm 63:1. First you read:

> O God, you are my God; earnestly I seek you;
>   my soul thirsts for you;
> my flesh faints for you,
>   as in a dry and weary land where there is no water.

Next you pray something like:

> God, thank you so much for being my God. I need you so badly. You are all that is good in this life and I cling to you. Forgive me for thirsting for other things instead of you.

Like the first method, this can be slow. A weakness of this method is our tendency to take control of the Psalm. If you are going to use this method, try to avoid the temptation of making your prayer more palatable than the psalm. This temptation becomes almost inescapable as psalms get harder to pray. God wants to see all the heat that's burning in our heart, and he provided the Psalms to graciously coax it out of us.

Praying through the Whole Psalter

Hopefully one or more of those methods will help you begin the ancient path to the presence of God. However, before we leave this "how to" chapter, we should consider how to pray through the Psalter as a whole. The easiest way is just to start with Psalm 1 and go through each one until you get to Psalm 150. "Then," as Joseph Letendre puts it, "go back to Psalm 1 and do it again. And again. Continue this for the rest of your life."[13] It really is that simple. You can pray whole psalms or a single verse, but eventually you want to pray through the whole book.

I have found that some kind of "system" helps me pray through the psalter, otherwise the whole thing becomes quite daunting. Three systems in particular, come to mind. First there is the 30-day cycle of prayers that is found in the early editions of the Book of Common Prayer. In this system, psalms are bunched into morning and evening readings such that you can open and close each day in psalmic prayer. (See the table on the opposite page.)

Thirty-Day Psalter

DAY	MORNING	EVENING
1	1–5	6–8
2	9–11	12–14
3	15–17	18
4	19–21	22–23
5	24–26	27–29
6	30–31	32–34
7	35–36	37
8	38–40	41–43
9	44–46	47–49
10	50–52	53–55
11	56–58	59–61
12	62–64	65–67
13	68	69–70
14	71–72	73–74
15	75–77	78
16	79–81	82–85
17	86–88	89
18	90–92	93–94
19	95–97	98–101
20	102–103	104
21	105	106
22	107	108–109
23	110–113	114–115
24	116–118	119:1–32
25	119:33–72	119:73–104
26	119:105–144	119:145–176
27	120–125	126–131
28	132–135	136–138
29	139–140	141–143
30	144–146	147–150

The second system is how I first began praying the Psalms. It offers the way to pray through the whole psalter in a month without the need to remember where you left off or rely on some outside grouping. On the first day of the month you pray Psalm 1, 31, 61, 91, 121. Each day of the month corresponds to the first Psalm you pray, and then you add thirty. You do that all the way to the 30th of the month, skipping Psalm 119. When a month has thirty-one days you pray Psalm 119 on that last day. This is a fine plan, but I quit using it because I wasn't learning the Psalter. It was too random. Praying sequentially helps me get a sense of the Psalter and comprehend the whole. In particular, many of the Psalms are clustered in groups and I missed seeing those unfold.

The third system has ended up being my favorite. It was created by Orthodox monks and has been a help to Christians around the world for centuries. It divides the Psalter into twenty sections (called *kathismata*). Each *kathisma* has three *stases.* If you have the time, you can pray a *kathisma* per day to get through the Psalter in twenty days. If you have less time, you can pray one *stasis* a day and get through all the Psalms in two months. I like this because like the one from the Book of Common Prayer, it is sequential. I enjoy getting to know the contours of the psalter, and how one psalm follows another—this is something you don't get with the previous system. I have the below table taped inside of my Bible so I can pray without looking anything up. I also like that it's easily broken up so you could pray a *stasis* every morning, noon, and night.

The *Kathismata* Psalter

	STASIS 1	STASIS 2	STASIS 3
1	1–3	4–6	7–8
2	9–11	12–14	15–17
3	18	19–21	22–24
4	25–27	28–30	31–32
5	33–34	35–36	37
6	38–40	41–43	44–46
7	47–49	50–51	52–55
8	56–58	59–61	62–64
9	65–67	68	69–70
10	71–72	73–74	75–77
11	78	79–81	82–85
12	86–88	89	90–91
13	92–94	95–97	98–101
14	102–103	104	105
15	106	107	108–109
16	110–112	113–116:9	116:10–118
17	119:1–72	119:73–131	119:32–176
18	120–124	125–129	130–134
19	135–137	138–140	141–143
20	144–145	146–147	148–150

I have left a lot of questions unanswered. Over the course of this book, we will consider how to pray different kinds of psalms and explore the Psalter for the spirituality it creates. We can pray the Psalms every day for the rest of our lives and we will meet God every time. Sometimes we will feel like we met him, other times we won't. Sometimes we will pray them out of need, and other times we will pray them out of sheer obedience. As we pray, though, we will wrestle with God in ways we thought impossible and will gradually be formed into the image of his Son.

What I've tried to provide in this chapter is a simple explanation to get you started. I hope to share other things that are helpful, but the most important thing you can do is just start praying the Psalms for yourself.

Getting to know God takes a lifetime and, like any meaningful relationship, you will know him better in twenty years than you do today. However, there are no shortcuts, special sayings, or special knowledge to get you there. One of my greatest regrets is the amount of time I spent reading books *about* spirituality rather than pursuing God himself. I wasted decades of my life reading spiritual books and imitating those people who actually met God. I was faking spirituality instead of practicing it. And I was wrong. It wasn't until I put those books down and started regularly talking to the actual person of God, that I did, in fact, meet God. Simply reading about psalmic prayer in this book will not bring you one bit closer to your Lord. You have to go meet him for yourself, but now you at least know how to navigate his ancient path.

Reflection 3: Praying the Psalms

Praying Psalm 138

It is time to try your hand at praying a psalm. We have tried it a little already in previous chapters, but now is the chance to explore your options. We will begin with Psalm 138, which is printed below.

This is my favorite psalm to use as I teach this practice. It is a generic psalm, in that it's not tied to an occasion and it covers multiple topics. In fact, this little psalm is like a mini psalter. Pray it and you will encounter many of the subjects that fill the rest of the book.

Psalm 138 begins with a compelling picture of the believer praising the Lord in the midst of other gods. That's the life of faith, isn't it? Especially in this secular world or ours. Even within our hearts we seek after God in the midst of idols. The psalm never really leaves this image, as it encourages us to pray in the midst of a world that doesn't know God.

From there, it begins the various prayers you will see elsewhere in the Psalter. Psalm 138 describes the act of worship, something we discussed in the previous chapter. In verse two, you can almost feel the psalm placing you in the posture of worship. It trains you like a coach, teaching a technique. Verse three makes reference to past deliverances, something that will figure prominently throughout the Psalter and our exploration of it.

It then goes on to make bold, almost cosmic requests—about kings of the earth becoming worshipers. Psalmic prayer will never let you tiptoe in the presence of God. Whether it's praying for one thing or against another, the Psalms hardly ever lack confidence. As Psalm 138 nears its end, it breaks the world into two categories: those God protects and those he counts as enemies. Get used to this kind of prayer. We will learn how to pray these kinds of prayers in later chapters but try your hand at it now.

The psalm pictures us as lowly, surrounded by foes, but delivered by the Lord. Notice that it is trying to set your worldview. It is what we talked about throughout Chapter 2. Maybe you don't feel lowly or surrounded but enter the spiritual environment of the psalm anyway. Let these things be true in your heart even if you aren't experiencing them at this very moment. In other words, let the psalm lead you into that perspective. By the end of the psalm, you will have no hope except the promise that God will not forsake the work of his hands. That is our actual reality, whether we acknowledge it or not.

Now it's time to pray this psalm to God. Practice what you have learned in this chapter. Pray it slowly and then pray it fast. This is a chance to see what you like. Try chanting it or listening to it. Because Psalm 138 is direct speech, you don't really have to choose between the first two methods that I have described. Simply pray the words as written, but practice *meaning* them and not just *reading* them. Meet God in this psalm, for his presence saturates the words.

I give you thanks, O Lord, with my whole heart;
  before the gods I sing your praise;
I bow down toward your holy temple
  and give thanks to your name for your steadfast love
    and your faithfulness,
  for you have exalted above all things your name
    and your word.

On the day I called, you answered me;
    my strength of soul you increased.
All the kings of the earth shall give you thanks, O Lord,
    for they have heard the words of your mouth,
and they shall sing of the ways of the Lord,
    for great is the glory of the Lord.
For though the Lord is high, he regards the lowly,
    but the haughty he knows from afar.
Though I walk in the midst of trouble,
    you preserve my life;
you stretch out your hand against the wrath of my enemies,
    and your right hand delivers me.
The Lord will fulfill his purpose for me;
    your steadfast love, O Lord, endures forever.
Do not forsake the work of your hands.

Part 2

The Psalmic Experience

Chapter 4

Choosing to Believe

In Part 1, the basic principles of psalmic prayer were introduced, both what is meant by praying the Psalms and how to do it. In Part 2, the spirituality we encounter as we pray different kinds of psalms will be the focus. Psalmic spirituality is quite different from most forms of modern spirituality, and that means that some of the Psalter's most prominent features might be challenging for us to put into practice. For me, there was a pretty steep learning curve to this kind of prayer. Hopefully sharing some insights might shorten that curve for you.

This is the point where most books about the Psalter begin categorizing psalms by topic, as if what we really need is a good filing system. In general, I am wary of this. I have yet to find a psalm that fits neatly into a single category, and I find it unpleasant to decide what a psalm is before encountering it in prayer. In fact, you will find that your impression of most every psalm will change over time, as its meaning grows, or your need for it evolves. I also believe that having categories only encourages us to cherry pick the Psalms, something that severely limits our psalmic experience. Knowing just the right psalm to pray will sometimes come in handy, but getting stretched by an unexpected psalm will be far more rewarding.

Instead of exploring the different categories of psalms, we will explore the different kinds of experiences we have as we pray them. Each psalm takes us through a different experience with God. Sometimes, the psalms will seem as contradictory as human experience, but that's part of the Psalter's charm. One psalm will encourage you to quietly trust God regardless of your situation, while another may question God aggressively because of it. Even the proximity psalms may seem incongruent. Psalm 87, for example, prances about as if Zion were the envy of the world, while Psalm 88 spirals into the darkest hell.

This experiential dimension is more helpful than the sanitized categories of the typical psalm study. Those categories make the Psalms sound like they belong in a scientific lab rather than the chaotic world of a prayer closet. We will touch on some traditional categories as we go, but we will mostly consider those spiritual features that are too broad or too subtle to fit nicely into a single package.

It is one of these broad-but-subtle features that begins our discussion. The first thing we will consider is the experience of belief. Most of us probably think of belief in terms of believing particular doctrines, like the deity of Christ or the atonement. In the Psalter, however, belief is more immersive and existential. In fact, belief is the fundamental experience behind each and every psalm, so it is a wonderful place to begin our exploration of the Psalter.

The Natural and the Supernatural

David's victory over Goliath is one of the high points of the Old Testament. While the world looks at this story and sees an inspiring tale, people of faith see nothing short of a miracle. God went to war that day. Little did Goliath know that he faced God rather than David. Because of that, Goliath was the one outmatched in the valley of Elah, not David. The smallness of God's instrument simply underscored God's power. It was a moment charged with supernatural overtones.

David's speech in front of Goliath is one of the greatest in all the Bible. "You come to me with a sword and with a spear and with a javelin, but I come to you in the name of the LORD of hosts, the God of the armies of Israel, whom you have defied" (1 Samuel 17:45). David was the tip of the Lord's spear and the extension of his will. I highly doubt that David would step onto the battlefield if he didn't believe God was fighting alongside him. This wasn't a story of strength meeting strength, this was a story of faith and deliverance. It is so extraordinary that we are hard-pressed to see anything other than divine intervention.

Compare that, however, with the events that took place in 1 Samuel 21. By that point, things were decidedly less supernatural. David stumbled into the tabernacle and swindled the priest out of some bread and Goliath's sword. Immediately after, David arrived in Gath, which was Goliath's hometown. The people of Gath were terrified of David. They had heard rumors that he killed thousands of warriors, and they certainly would have recognized

Goliath's sword at his side. Little did they know that this was a very different David. This was a hobo. The man who once led armies now schemed to stay alive. And, in one of the Bible's more pitiful moments, David changed his behavior so the people of Gath wouldn't come near him. As Samuel says it, David "made marks on the doors of the gate and let his spittle run down his beard" (1 Samuel 21:13).

The Gath story is as spiritually anemic as the Goliath story had been vibrant. Watching David survive by charade is painful, and it's hard not to think that David had lost faith in the Lord. We get no sense that David was chosen by God or was being directed by him. David never prayed for deliverance or announced the power of God. He even managed to break a few commandments along the way. First Samuel 21 is just a story of a person on his own, a story that could be about anyone in the ancient world. The God that fought at David's side in the valley of Elah is a distant memory.

Yet this isn't how David saw it. He let the spittle run down his beard and then wrote a psalm that expressed God's care for his children and his power to save. Never mind that God's care and his power are two things that appear to be absent in the actual story. It's hard to imagine anything spiritual coming from such an unspiritual ordeal, but the events of 1 Samuel 21 were actually the inspiration for one the great psalms of deliverance.[14] Here are some highlights from it.

The angel of the LORD encamps
around those who fear him,
and delivers them. *Psalm 34:7*

The young lions suffer want and hunger;
but those who seek the LORD
lack no good thing. *Psalm 34:10*

Keep your tongue from evil
and your lips from speaking deceit. *Psalm 34:13*

When the righteous cry for help,
the Lord hears
and delivers them out of all their troubles.
The LORD is near to the brokenhearted
and saves the crushed in spirit.
Many are the afflictions of the righteous,
but the LORD delivers him out of them all.
He keeps all his bones;
not one of them is broken. *Psalm 34:17–20*

Psalm 34 casts a natural event in a supernatural light. In fact, David sounds like he is describing a moment with as much spiritual significance and moral clarity as the Goliath event. David is radiant, not a beggar. God is vigilant, not silent. In Psalm 34 the righteous never lack food and never lie or deceive. Ironically, in 1 Samuel 21, David did both. David, however, is oblivious to the irony; faith usually is. It's as if he saw one thing with his eyes but something different with his heart. I wonder if he would be embarrassed if he knew that believers in our day knew what really happened in Gath. If I were David, it would embarrass me.

Once, while backpacking in the Ozark Mountains, I rounded a corner and came face-to-face with a bear. The bear stood on his hind legs and my heart dropped to my feet. But I was an experienced hiker and knew how to handle that situation: I made noise and walked away as casually as possible. When I told friends of my little adventure, I handled it differently than David. I was glad that I didn't die, but I wasn't going to make it more spiritual than it was. It was a black bear not a grizzly, so it is basically an oversized raccoon. And I handled the whole thing myself. I gave God less credit rather than more. That's my usual way. I only let God have his miracles when miracles are the only option left.

But my outlook on life had to change when I started praying the Psalms. The spiritual exuberance of Psalm 34 is normal in the Psalter. When we pray the Psalms, we regularly speak to God as if we are his top priority, literally the apple of his eye (Psalm 17:8). The Psalms force us to speak as if our life circumstances are the spot where the eternal scales are being weighed. If you *study* the Psalms instead of praying them, you don't have to take part in this exaggeration. You can observe, take note, then dismiss. Our goal, however, is to enter their spiritual environment. We want to participate alongside them by letting their words become our words. And psalmic words are dramatic. Whether we like it or not, their supernatural drama becomes our supernatural drama.

The Psalms will not let you draw the line between what you have done on your own and what the Lord has done on your behalf. That line doesn't exist in the Psalter. For some Christians, that will be a comfort because they know that God is active and near, so the Psalter will give voice to how they already see the world. For other Christians, ones like myself, praying the Psalms challenges the very core of our cynical worldview. The Psalms assume that an all-powerful God can and will do all-powerful things. The Psalms assume that God is always at the ready and is an active participant in our lives.

God as an Active Participant

My wife loves to tell a story that is similar, but different, from my story about the bear. It's a story about angels protecting her from a bike wreck. She was headed down a steep hill and was going too fast to make the turn at the bottom. Inexplicably, though, she made the turn. Those are all the facts of the story, but for the past twenty years she has insisted that an angel protected her. Neither of us saw any angels, but she believes it nonetheless. She *chooses* to believe. There is no other way to say it. Time might wear down her memory of the details, but it will never hinder her ongoing decision to believe that God was an active participant in it.

This brings us to the very heart of psalmic spirituality. David's spiritual retelling of 1 Samuel 21 seems naive, if not foolish, but it is a retelling that is drenched in faith. It is saturated in the idea that God is active in even the most unexceptional things. This faith in

God's activity is the underlying principle of the Psalter. It is the reason that Psalm 34 sounds as spiritual as it does. And, as you pray the Psalms, you will find this idea everywhere. You will hear it in the exaggerated requests, where the psalmist asks God to bow his heavens just to deliver his child. You will notice it when the psalmist throws a temper tantrum, laying out unrealistic expectations as he holds God's feet to the fire. No matter the subject, the Psalms teach an unwavering belief that God is responsible for the events of this life. The Psalms express faith even as they verbalize doubt.

This faith, however, is a decision that we have to make. There may only be a few times in life when God is so active that there can be no other explanation. That means that we will usually have to decide what we believe without stacks of overwhelming evidence. The Psalms, meanwhile, don't try to provide that evidence. They don't transform our external experience, instead they reconfigure our perspective of it. They do this by having us rehearse the spiritual reality in prayer. Through psalmic prayer, we practice having a supernatural worldview.

You may simply be on your morning commute, but the Psalter will have you praying like you are going to meet Goliath. You may be getting your kids ready for church, but you can pray the same prayers Jesus prayed before the Mount of Transfiguration. The Psalms won't try to convince you that you are as historically important as David and Jesus, but they will try to convince you that you have the same God. They will convince you that he loves you as much as he loved them. No matter how small our lives may seem, we have the same prayer book as the king of Israel and the King of kings!

The more I have prayed through the Psalms, the more I have noticed David's tendency to turn events like 1 Samuel 21 into prayers like Psalm 34. It's easy to read the Psalms and think he was always being persecuted for righteousness's sake, but I'm not sure we could tell. He prayed the same regardless of whether he is doing "holy" work or not. Certainly the king of Israel was the Lord's anointed, but some of his complaints are problems we could find in Washington DC just as easily as ancient Jerusalem. There was palace intrigue, political infighting, false accusations, and personal betrayals. Psalm 35 is a great example.

> Malicious witnesses rise up;
> they ask me of things that I do not know.
> They repay me evil for good;
> My soul is bereft. (vv. 11–12)

In Psalm 35, David had a moment of weakness and his supposed friends took advantage of that and betrayed him. That's just another day at the office for a political leader, but David prayed like he was still standing in the valley of Elah; like he was still opposing Goliath. The God that was with him on that battlefield was the same God he called upon in partisan politics. Listen to him summon the Lord from the same psalm.

> Take hold of shield and buckler
> and rise for my help!

Draw the spear and javelin
against my pursuers!
Say to my soul,
"I am your salvation!" (vv. 2–3)

Our life will rarely match the intensity of the Psalter's prayers. How often are you so tormented by others that you are ready for God to draw his spear against your enemies? How regularly can you praise God that none of your bones are broken? But David's experiences weren't all that different from our own. The events behind Psalms 34 and 35 show us that. David wasn't always fighting a giant, but he always prayed like he was.

Perhaps David didn't see a difference between what happened with Goliath and what happened in Gath. Perhaps that's why he had the guts to fight Goliath in the first place. Perhaps David simply had a radical sense that God was participating in the daily activities of his saints and, if that was the case, then the day he met Goliath was just like any other day. David didn't need an extra dose of God or even an extra dose of prayer. He wasn't rising to the occasion. David was merely doing the obvious thing given his assumptions about God. Whatever was on the other end of his sling didn't matter.

He admitted as much when he was about to fight Goliath. Turning down the armor that was being offered he said, "The Lord who delivered me from the paw of the lion and from the paw of the bear will deliver me from the hand of this Philistine" (1 Samuel 17:37). Whether it was lions, or bears, or giants, David was motivated by the one he served, not by the one he faced. In a strange way, this flattened out David's perspective, such that Goliath and Gath were much the same. For those of us who spend our days catastrophizing about life events, David's detachment is wonderfully refreshing. David simply believed that God was carrying him like a man carries his son and would fight for him at all costs. That wasn't David over-spiritualizing. That was David believing the Bible (Deuteronomy 1:30–31).

Deciding to Believe

As we pray the Psalms, we enter a different ecosystem. We live in that world through prayer, breathing in its supernatural environment. But it is a hidden world, different from the rest of our experiences. In the psalmic world, rivers flow where God wants them to and where lions seek their food from his hand. In the Psalter, the word of the Lord isn't just about preaching and learning, the word is proclaimed by the heavens, melts the snow, and helps the deer give birth. As we pray the Psalms, we orient our life around the fact that God, as Psalm 36 says, is the fountain of life.

These are hard prayers to pray because they are hard truths to believe. God's presence and activity are camouflaged by the materialism of everyday life. In fact, it's so well disguised that even we Christians forget.

When my oldest daughter was still a toddler, she woke up from a nap and couldn't walk. Her leg had feeling, but she couldn't move it. My wife frantically called me on her way to the doctor and immediately, I started to pray. I pleaded that God would heal my daughter. When I arrived at the doctor's office, there was my daughter running around in circles. I would love to tell you that I erupted into praises to my God, but I didn't. The first emotion I felt was embarrassment. I thought about how our reaction looked like the overreaction of first-time parents. We weren't having an emergency, she probably just slept funny. I think I even apologized for bringing her in.

I hate that story. I hate it because of what it said about me. I chose a natural explanation because I never spent time in that ecosystem of God. Doctrinally speaking, I believed in a world where God fed the lions and found nests for baby birds, yet when pressed, I chose a world without God. We live in an era where humans and technology wield limitless power, and surely that is affecting our spirituality. I know it has affected mine.

If that situation with my daughter happened today, I would like to think that I might handle it differently. As we discussed in Chapter 2, praying the Psalms gives us better spiritual reflexes. I am less quick to draw a line between what is and isn't God's work. I am more willing to accept the foolishness that comes with believing. In short, I am more willing to leap into that world where God sends angels on bike rides. I can assure you that such a world is a happier place.

It is so difficult to *know* the ordinary but *believe* the extra-ordinary. We can see our bank account and touch our resume. We can take our medicine and climb a social ladder. That is our normal, visible, un-supernatural life. But hidden within that life is the hand of God. He stands at the ready as an active participant in the lives of his saints. He is on the other side of the veil, just beyond our sight, and the Psalter helps train our eyes to see him.

When David offered his final retrospective on his life in Psalm 18, it was a raucous celebration of the power and activity of God. David was a mess at times, sinning with the worst of them, but his prayers are those of someone convinced that God was an enthusiastic Deliverer. As David reminisced about his life, he remembered how God moved heaven and earth whenever David called for help.

> Then the earth reeled and rocked;
>   the foundations also of the mountains trembled
>   and quaked, because he was angry.
> Smoke went up from his nostrils,
>   and devouring fire from his mouth;
>   glowing coals flamed forth from him.
> He bowed the heavens and came down;
>   thick darkness was under his feet. (Psalm 18:7–9)

None of this probably happened physically, but it was happening behind the veil. And who is to say that what happens behind the veil is any less real than what happens on this side of it? Who's to say that this isn't exactly what happened? David was a dead shot with a sling in his hand, but it was God who delivered him from Goliath. David slobbered his way out of Gath, but it was God who encamped around him. David's accusers fell into the traps they had made for him, but God was executing justice. God was a thundering force in David's life and, by praying the Psalms, we decide that he's a thundering force in ours.

Reflection 4: Praying Like a Child

Praying Psalm 131

I've mentioned that prayer is not easy for me. My love of psalmic prayer comes from a place of weakness, rather than one of strength. I need God to supply words for me to pray because I might not pray otherwise. In fact, *not* praying has been an embarrassing mark of my Christian life. I tried everything to jumpstart my prayer life. I read great books by faithful pray-ers, like George Muller and Andrew Murray, which only buried me in guilt. I read the amazing book (*A Praying Life*) by Paul Miller, which was more helpful than others but the changes didn't last. I also tried my hand at contemplative prayer, only to discover that I was more contemplative than I was prayerful.

There were plenty of problems that led to my struggles, not the least of which was my trying to get better at prayer by reading books rather than praying. But the problems always seemed more stubborn than my solutions. Even as I planted a church, I struggled. If ever there was a time to pray, it's when you plant a church. Church planters have crazy spiritual experiences—even Presbyterian ones—but my prayer life only flickered with occasional signs of life. It wasn't until I was praying regularly that I could look back and diagnose my situation. One problem stood above the rest, and it's spelled out in Psalm 131.

> O LORD, my heart is not lifted up;
> my eyes are not raised too high;
> I do not occupy myself with things
> too great and too marvelous for me. (v. 1)

I struggled to pray because of a pesky humanism that always lifted up my heart and eyes too high, which meant that I was always occupied with things too great and too marvelous for me. Prayer in those days meant bowing my head and being overwhelmed. There was so much to do with a young family and a church plant that I either didn't have time to pray or my mind raced too fast for the pace of prayer. My problems seemed too big to condense into the human language, much less a single prayer. And if I couldn't communicate my problems, how could I pray at all? There were so many times I tried to pray but simply froze instead.

It didn't occur to me that those were the best times to pray. I thought prayer was having things figured out enough to ask God for help. I assumed my job was to articulate the problem and God's job was to solve it, as if we were having some cosmic board meeting. I thought prayer depended on me and my control of a situation. Of course, I didn't know at the time that this was happening but, looking back, it is obvious. And it was such a pervasive theme that I might as well admit it here. I'm never so optimistic that I think I can do everything, but I am humanistic enough to think I should. Hearts that are lifted up that high are never hearts that pray.

Psalm 131 challenges our pesky humanism. It pictures a child that looks no higher than his mother. Sure, there are problems aplenty, but that's none of the child's business. Those problems are too big for him. He doesn't raise his eyes that high and isn't concerned with such great and marvelous things. After all, he is just a child. Imagine what it would be like if this child thought he could solve adult-sized problems. It's preposterous, as preposterous as humans thinking we can solve God-sized problems. Imagine what would happen if he tried! It would be a disaster. So he looks to his mother and is glad that she's the mom and he's the child.

Insufficiency produces prayer while self-sufficiency kills it. The ignorant call out for wisdom, the weak for strength, the broken for healing, the empty for filling, and the fearful for safety. It's as if we were intentionally made to be jars of clay, so that whatever we end up becoming is a credit to God and not to us (2 Corinthians 4:7). Maybe that's why we boast about our weaknesses, because weakness is where we find the Lord.

If David taught us anything in Gath, it's that life is a subtle miracle. Even when David was scheming, he saw God as an active participant. Anyone can be in over their head when facing Goliath, but it's quite another thing to be in over our head when our plans work exactly as we expected. This makes Psalm 34 all the more remarkable. Physically speaking, the problems in Gath were well within David's ability, but he chose to be a weaned child in the midst of his sufficiency. The active participation of God gave David permission to always be out of his depth, regardless of whether he was acting the fool or standing over the giant's corpse.

The Psalms are melodramatic. In upcoming chapters, we will see how they fling themselves from one extreme to another. I used to think these histrionics were the result of poetic passion, but the more I pray the Psalms the more I have realized that there is a child at the center of the Psalter. That child is constantly faced with situations too great and too marvelous. That child is not as passionate as he is overwhelmed. The Psalms will never encourage you to feel adequate within yourself. They will never teach you to weather your own storm or fight your own battles. They outsource every human experience, bringing them to the throne of God. The Psalter is the toddler of the Bible.

Praying the Psalms means learning to be less self-sufficient. It means becoming a child. For some, this will be our greatest spiritual challenge. The goal is to lift our hearts and eyes less high and be less concerned with things so great and marvelous. We can either learn that lesson by hitting rock bottom or we can let psalmic prayer teach us how to live that way. The latter is less painful.

Once I discovered my habit of concerning myself with things too great and too marvelous for me, I used Psalm 131 to help retrain my mind. For years I recited that psalm before my prayer time. It was a constant reminder that I didn't have it figured out and that

I didn't have to. It redirected my gaze: from my problems to my God. I encourage you to do the same. Use this psalm as a motto for your time with God. Recite it before you speak with him. Make it a short prayer you pray when the pressures rise at work or at home. Having this outlook doesn't mean you shrug and do nothing. David did plenty in his life, but he did what he did with an inner child that was dependent on his parent.

As we leave this chapter, think about a problem in your life and prayerfully meditate on Psalm 131:1. Feel free to think about life's biggest problem or, better yet, choose a problem you know you can solve on your own. Then, for a few moments, simply be overwhelmed by it. Let God give you comfort even if you don't totally need it. Put your head on God's chest and be glad that he is the parent and you are the child. It is only then that we can have the calm and quiet of that weaned child. Too often we read Psalm 131 and try to find the peace of that child without first becoming that child. Too often we want to cast our anxieties on the Lord (1 Peter 5:7) without first humbling ourselves under his mighty hand (1 Peter 5:6). Pray Psalm 131 now and discover the peace that comes from prayer.

Chapter 5

The Rock of Our Refuge

By 587 BC, most of the promised land had already been carved up by foreign powers. Judah, the last vestige of God's original society, found itself on the brink of collapse as Babylonian forces invaded and destroyed Jerusalem. The book of Lamentations recounts the events in shocking detail. Bodies lay in the streets and the living resembled the dead. Mothers, who dearly loved their children, were forced to eat them to stay alive. It was a terror for any person unfortunate enough to be left alive.

Psalm 74 is one of the great Psalms of Asaph, and it tries to make sense of these atrocities. It pictures the Babylonians as wild boars, running berserk through the streets of the holy city. Foreign soldiers, whose very presence was profane, swung axes in the temple like lumberjacks. The temple burned, the enemy roared, and God was silent. "How could that be?" the psalmist asks. How could God, who can break the heads of sea monsters and crush the Leviathan, let such things happen to his own people?

> How long, O God, is the foe to scoff?
> Is the enemy to revile your name forever?
> Why do you hold back your hand, your right hand?
> Take it from the fold of your garment and destroy them! (Psalm 74:10–11)

We can hear the bewilderment of God's people. God could deliver his people with a flick of his wrist, so why wasn't he? Why was he holding back? Why wouldn't God direct his steps to the heap of ruins that used to be his sanctuary? Psalm 74 has a clarity that only comes with desperation: if God would not save Judah, then Judah could not be saved.

When we are under duress, we fly like a bird to our refuge, and one of the greatest themes in the Psalter is how God can be that refuge for us. Fleeing to God sounds easy enough, but it isn't that simple. With every crisis comes the temptation to find our refuge somewhere else. In our modern age, most of us rely on ourselves. We rely on our own strength and understanding; we assess our weaknesses and make up for them in other ways. The Psalter, however, challenges us to do otherwise. It challenges us to look outside ourselves and hide in the presence of God.

In this chapter we explore what it means to find our refuge in God. Psalm 74 will be our guide, because it may be one of the most extraordinary prayers of deliverance in all the Psalter. The psalm itself is standard, but its context makes it unique. Psalm 74 teaches us to flee to God when we are most likely to look to ourselves.

A Prayer of Deliverance

If you have read much of the Old Testament, you probably know why the Babylonians are in the streets of Jerusalem. Several prophets had repeatedly warned of the invasion, calling it God's judgment. Going all the way back to Moses, God promised that disobedience meant foreign armies "swooping down like the eagle" (Deuteronomy 28:15, 49–50). In other words, the people should have known the extent of their sin, the degree of God's anger, and the power of those who were coming. In the book of Habakkuk, even God seems impressed with the Babylonian (Chaldean) army.

> For I am doing a work in your days
>   that you would not believe if told.
> For behold, I am raising up the Chaldeans,
>   that bitter and hasty nation,
> who march through the breadth of the earth,
>   to seize dwellings not their own.
> They are dreaded and fearsome;
>   their justice and dignity go forth from themselves.
> Their horses are swifter than leopards,
>   more fierce than the evening wolves;
>   their horsemen press proudly on.
> Their horsemen come from afar;
>   they fly like an eagle swift to devour.
>
> (Habakkuk 1:5–8)

By the time Babylon started swooping down, God was so angry with his people that he planned to "wipe Jerusalem as one wipes a dish." The Lord continues, "I will forsake the remnant of my heritage and give them into the hand of their enemies, and they shall become a prey and a spoil to all their enemies" (2 Kings 21:13–14). In other words, God's people deserved it. There had been generations of sin with only occasional obedience. One king in particular (Manasseh) had "burned his son as an offering and used fortune-telling and omens and dealt with mediums and with necromancers" (2 Kings 21:6).

As God's anger burned hot, what kind of prayer would God want his people to pray? This was a sinful group of people getting the punishment they deserved. They had no excuse, which makes Psalm 74 all the more surprising. It is a prayer for *deliverance* rather than a prayer of *confession*. Of course, the people needed to confess their sins, and other Psalms of Asaph provide that opportunity (Psalm 50, 78). But God didn't want his people to stay in the confession-phase of redemption. He wanted them to confess their sin and move on.

Psalm 74 assesses the power of Babylon and the silence of God, and that's it. It doesn't ask whether the people learned their lesson or will do better, it simply cries out in a time of trial. I cannot stress enough that this prayer was prayed *during* that time of trial. Babylonians were still running through the streets, which meant God's people were still in the midst of their punishment. Does this surprise you? It does me.

Psalm 74 almost seems negligent, at least compared to modern spirituality. There is no angst over the sin, only angst over the punishment. Psalm 74 completely disregards the reason for the Babylonian invasion. I can hardly get my head around this. We are born wallowers, but Psalm 74 makes me wonder if that is what God wants from us. It makes me wonder whether wallowing in our guilt is just a way for us to turn inward and find our refuge within ourselves.

Imagine standing before God, covered in the stench of your own sin, and asking him to fix some problem that you created. Let's say you are fully guilty and suffering the obvious consequences. How do you pray through that experience? How long do you confess? I tend to confess as long as I feel guilty; certainly I will confess my sin as long as I think I'm being punished for it. And do you turn inward? Do you try to fix it on your own? Do you bear God's discipline quietly, like we think a pious Christian should? Or worse, do you punish yourself for your sin? If any of this is the case, and I suspect it is, then we are handling our situation differently than Psalm 74 teaches.

Psalm 71:3 prays to the Lord, "Be to me a rock of refuge, to which I may continually come." God wants to be our refuge *continually*, for all occasions. Many of us, however, feel the need to do a bit of pre-deliverance before asking for deliverance. That means we aren't really letting God do the delivering. In Psalm 74, the bodies were still in the street and smoke still lingered in the air, but God's children came running. They came to him even when their own guilt was still hot on their tail.

God wants to be our deliverer, pure and simple. He wants to be the solution to every one of our problems, regardless of the cause. God's people still had to endure his punishment. The Babylonians triumphed and Judah went into exile, but God wanted them to seek deliverance throughout that phase of their life. He wanted them to look outward rather than inward. That's the core teaching of Psalm 74 as I understand it, and it is a prominent feature throughout the rest of the Psalter. We must come running to God while we are guilty, or we will never come running at all. Psalm 74 is a case study of this spiritual experience.

The God of Our Mess

We have a rule in our home that everyone should clean up after themselves. If it's yours, pick it up. In our family, if your friend is coming over then you must do most of the cleaning. I love my children, but I'm not going to walk around and do what they can do for themselves. Apparently, that is not how it works in the kingdom of God. You can make a complete mess of your life and still ask God to clean it up.

Throughout the Psalter, our relationship with God is not based on whether we are clean, but whether we cry out. Psalm 50, which is the closest thing to God screaming at his children, offers an immediate fix to the broken relationship. God's love is offered quickly, quickly enough to give us spiritual whiplash.

> Mark this, then, you who forget God,
> lest I tear you apart, and there be none to deliver!
> The one who offers thanksgiving as his sacrifice glorifies me;
> to one who orders his way rightly
> I will show the salvation of God! (vv. 22–23)

In just a few lines, God goes from almost tearing his people apart to showing them his salvation. This is the kind of God we serve. How quick the Lord is to forgive and reinstate, and how slow we are to forgive ourselves. All God wants in Psalm 50 is for his people to simply be thankful and try. It is a low bar. God will pivot quicker than we can finish a prayer. We don't have to pay extra and there is nothing for us to fix.

We, on the other hand, are prone to demand more of ourselves. We wait until we feel forgiven or withhold our joy until we act better. I don't mean to spoil the story, but Judah didn't learn much from the Babylonian invasion. After years in captivity, they came back and started sinning as if they had never left. Yet God did not withhold a prayer like Psalm 74 until they could prove themselves faithful. He simply wanted them to cry out to him.

Praying Angry

The grace of Psalm 74 says that we can stand knee-deep in blood and ash but still petition a holy God. Being guilty is no reason to keep our distance. We can come running. But that is just the beginning. Psalm 74 goes further, because God's grace goes further. Let's take a second look at Psalm 74:

> How long, O God, is the foe to scoff?
> Is the enemy to revile your name forever?
> Why do you hold back your hand, your right hand?
> Take it from the fold of your garment and destroy
> them! (vv. 10–11)

There are accusations embedded within this psalm. "How long?" the psalmist asks. Is God not paying attention? Is God not delivering the people that he promised to deliver? The Babylonians ran through the streets because Judah polluted herself, yet the psalmist called God to account. Verse 9 is almost laughable: "Do not deliver the soul of your dove to the wild beasts."

Your dove! That seems a bit tone deaf. It wasn't as if Judah had spent the last hundred years in prayer and worship. Ezekiel described some pretty un-dove-like behavior: "you trusted in your beauty and played the whore because of your renown and lavished your whorings on any passerby!" (Ezekiel 16:15) Meanwhile the psalmist has the audacity to picture Judah as a dove and God as silent. That imagery begs the question: what kind of a God wouldn't save an innocent dove?

Psalm 74 continues by claiming that God failed to notice the scoffing and reviling of sinners. This feels like hypocrisy. Judah had turned scoffing and reviling into a national pastime. The psalm even reminds God not to forget the life of his poor, even though God's people oppressed the poor and needy, extorting those who sojourned in their country. Psalm 77, another Psalm of Asaph, goes even further.[15] It is almost cruel:

> Has [God's] steadfast love forever ceased?
> Are his promises at an end for all time?
> Has God forgotten to be gracious? (vv. 8–9)

These prayers are ruthless, but not sinful. The psalmist is fully convinced of the power of God, and he has unflinching faith in his promise. These psalms are comparing the plight of God's people to the promises the Lord had made. The two were not measuring up and the psalmist railed against it. The psalmist held God's feet to the fire as a natural outworking of his faith. It's angry faith, but faith nonetheless. The psalmist is shaking his fist at God because God seems to be neglecting his side of the bargain. Israel wasn't chosen because of something within themselves, it was always the result of God's promise, so the psalmist has a right to call him to account (Deuteronomy 7:7, 9:5).

God's steadfast love will never cease. His promises will never fail. God will never forget to be gracious. It's ridiculous to even have to say that, but reading these angry psalms could lead someone to wonder. God's steadfast love in truth runs so deep that he would allow us to question his character in the midst of our moral failures. His promises are so strong that we are invited to use them as leverage against God in prayer. I believe the point of these prayers is that God would rather us question him than question ourselves. He wants us to come running *to* him even if it means running *at* him.

I also believe that God gave us these prayers just to get us talking. There are times when my daughters are so angry that they can't articulate why. When it starts to reach a boiling point, I sometimes push them with enough questions that their anger spills over. It starts out directed at me, but I do it because they need a safe place to vent their anger. We have a pretty peaceful household, and children typically fear disrupting the vibe of their family. I fear the moment when my daughters go into their room and spiral. I would rather them be mad at me than close themselves off. So I provoke them to get them talking. They get going and their real problems come out. It is a tactic I learned from my heavenly Father and these angry psalms.

When we are struggling with sin and guilt, we need more than prayers of confession. We need to be rescued from ourselves. God does not want us to lock ourselves in our room alone and spiral, which is what many of us will do on our own. God's worst-case scenario is that we self-medicate by turning inward. He would rather us come out swinging than keep our distance until our problem is solved. Instead, God summons us out of the shadows of our sin. When we are weak and frail, the anger of Psalm 74 might be just what we need to start talking. God, in his wondrous grace, is willing to pick a fight.

Letting Go

Much of my spiritual life was an exercise in spiritual introspection. For years I sought to know myself and fix my own problems. I thought spirituality was a journey into the depths of my heart. It was an exhausting way to live because we can never know the depths of our own hearts. It is also a faithless way to live because the eyes of faith look to the Lord. Introspection and self-assessment are just religious ways to find refuge in ourselves. I needed out. I needed the freedom of the Psalms of Asaph.

As I prayed through the Psalter, I noticed that they hardly ever looked inward. As I mentioned in the previous chapter, the Psalms outsource human experience by laying it at the feet of the Lord. As we see in Asaph, the psalmist flings himself at the Lord with little regard for the depths of the human heart. Psalm 74 is an extreme example, but it captures the outward focus of the entire Psalter. Praying the Psalms taught me how to look at God and let him figure out the mess that is my heart. We are taught how to look outward throughout Scripture, but we may not have taken notice. We often recite the end of Psalm 139, but I invite you to reexamine it in the light of what we have seen.

> Search me, O God, and know my heart!
>   Try me and know my thoughts!
> And see if there be any grievous way in me,
>   and lead me in the way everlasting! (vv. 23–24)

Notice that it is God who does the searching, the testing, and the knowing. Yet we Christians spend countless hours searching ourselves and pretending to know our own hearts. We obsess about our motives because we buy into the modern misconception that we are neutral observers of ourselves. We try to fix our own flesh because we think that is what Christians are supposed to do. We think we are being vigilant, but we are in truth just denying God his proper place as the Searcher and Tester of our hearts.

The lesson of the Psalter is that we don't have to manage ourselves because we can be managed by God. We don't have to know ourselves because we can be known. We don't have to fortify ourselves because we can be strengthened. We don't have to prop ourselves up or prove ourselves to the world. We are free, free to come running to God.

Paul and the Freedom of Self-Forgetfulness

The church in Corinth had only been around for about five years by the time Paul wrote his first letter to the Corinthians. By that point, the church was already a disaster. There were fights between the advocates of Jewish law and the advocates for Christian freedom. Married couples had quit sleeping together, and the news broke that a man was sleeping with his stepmother. Some Christians were getting drunk together at communion while others were suing each other in civil court. Amidst all of that, false teachers came along and questioned whether Paul had the authority to address the church's problems. That means that Paul's Corinthian letters spend as much time defending the right to be read as they do confronting the mess that was Corinth.

Paul was under immense pressure to prove himself. He had reason to boast, of course. He had traveled the known world and had at least an inkling that his letters bore the weight of the word of God. Meanwhile, his life's work was on the verge of collapse because men of inferior skill and authority had polluted the church as soon as he left it. It must have been maddening. Paul was changing the world but was also being ground down by it. Yet surprisingly, in the very place we might expect to see him vouching for himself, Paul does something quite different. He declares himself free of himself and his need for introspection and self-approval:

> With me it is a very small thing that I should be judged by you or by any human court. In fact, I do not even judge myself. For I am not aware of anything against myself, but I am not thereby acquitted. It is the Lord who judges me. (1 Corinthians 4:3–4)

Paul cared for the Christians in Corinth. He was grieved that his harsh letters had caused them pain, and his concern for the churches was as burdensome to him as being shipwrecked, robbed, and beaten. Paul loved them, but that didn't mean he would allow himself to be judged by them. He saw the churches he planted as his recommendation to the world and his boast before the Lord. Somehow, though, he was able to let go of his achievements and need for self-reflection. Paul must have had Psalm 139 lingering somewhere in the back of his mind. He must have rehearsed this self-forgetfulness countless times in prayer.[16]

I long for this kind of freedom. I wish I could preach a sermon on Sunday and not spend the rest of the day ruminating on the good things I forgot to say, or kicking myself for the stupid things I wish I hadn't said. I've never had to defend my ministry like Paul did, yet I can't help but prance about when I do something moderately well and catastrophize when something doesn't go as planned. I have studied Paul's statement in 1 Corinthians diligently, hoping that I could learn enough about the gospel to experience its freedom. About the only thing I have learned is that gospel freedom isn't a matter of education.

When I think back on Psalm 74, I see a prayer that lets God do all the heavy lifting. The people who first prayed it experienced horrific conditions, but they were conditions that were outside of their control. They came running to God and let him sort out whether they were still guilty, whether they had confessed enough, and whether they would do better. Those were questions that they knew they could not answer. This was the kind of thinking that was grounds from Paul's greatest gospel declarations. It is no small spiritual practice.

Psalm 61:2 says, "Lead me to the rock that is higher than I." That is what Psalm 74 trains us to do. Praying this psalm, and the rest of the Psalter, can replace our self-obsessing thoughts with godward prayers. They can teach us that we are not the highest rock, that we don't have to be. It is God's job to search us, to know us, to test us, to deliver us, and to fix us. In that way, the Psalter will teach us how to be free.

Reflection 5: Hiding in the Presence of God

Praying Psalm 46

We can hardly talk about God being a refuge without ending the discussion in Psalm 46. It is one of the great psalms of the Bible, and the first line bursts with the exclamation: "God is our refuge and strength, a very present help in trouble." As we have seen in this chapter, we usually experience God as a refuge when we find ourselves in some kind of distress. And Psalm 46 has plenty of distress.

This psalm is a message of peace in the midst of a storm. The word "storm" hardly does the context justice, however, because what the psalm describes is a cataclysmic event that no human could withstand on their own. The earth gives way and mountains fall into the sea. Waves roar and water levels rise. Kingdoms shake and rage. Whatever real-world events inspired the psalmist, he feels like his world is being completely ripped apart. Psalm 46 has the feeling of vertigo, where everything is moving, shaking, and falling. It sounds miserable, if not terrifying.

In moments like this, we have to locate a fixed point, and Psalm 46 provides one. God is in his temple, says the psalmist, and the temple shall not be moved (v. 5). In fact, the Lord, and his unmoving presence, is the only thing *not* moving. God is our fixed point when everything else is in turmoil.

We have friends who own a sailboat, and they occasionally take us sailing in New York Harbor. Open water makes me a bit nervous but getting to see New York City from that vantage point is too great to pass up. Their advice to me was simply to keep looking at the horizon, because it is the one thing not moving. Even the big waves from a cruise ship can't affect the stability of dry land. So I locked my eyes on the horizon, focusing on the stable thing so that the moving things didn't swallow up my reality.

This is what Psalm 46 is: a reminder of our horizon. It is a call to lock onto it. Like a sea captain in the midst of a storm, God shouts his directions: "Be still, and know that I am God" (v. 10). That phrase is one of the most soothing in all the Bible, but it is delivered with urgency and at least a hint of rebuke. But that's what the psalmist needed. It's what we all need. We need to be snapped out of the chaos. God calls out to us, commands us even, because our world may be falling apart. And in all of that chaos and motion, God is the one thing not moving. He gathers us in so that we can hide with him as the storm passes by. He brings us into his presence so we can partake of his stillness.

Psalm 46:4–5 is a description of God's presence. It is a place where God's streams calm us and nourish us. I love the comparison of water in the psalm: God's tiniest streams are more powerful than the world's foaming waves. Psalm 46:8–9 reminds us to behold *God's* works, even when our world seems to crumble. It reminds me of Peter as he walked on the water. It was hard for him to keep his eyes on the Lord when the wind and waves were vying for his attention (Matthew 14:30). He got distracted and sank. We do the same. When God tells us to behold his works, he is telling us to expect more from his power as we experience the unrestrained power of this world.

Each one of us will find ourselves in one kind of storm or another. Like the psalmist in Psalm 46, it may be some kind of disaster that takes over our life. Or, like the psalmist in Psalm 74, we may have to endure the repercussions of our own sinful behavior. Whatever the cause, the solution is the same: run to God for refuge.

In this reflection, let's pray Psalm 46. You may be in a place of peace, so a prayer like this might be more preparation than triage. Or maybe you feel like the psalmist, where you are lashed by waves and scrambling up falling rocks. If that's the case, this psalm might need to be shouted. Either way, I encourage you to enter the peaceful presence of God's holy habitation. There is nothing but safety at the feet of our Lord. There is stillness, not motion.

When I was growing up, the kids in my neighborhood sometimes played a street-wide game of hide-and-seek. Getting caught meant having to outrun everyone who had already been caught and, eventually, it meant getting tackled. I was the youngest and smallest of the group, so finding a place to hide was a concern of great interest. I still remember the mad dash and the panic. Then, during one particular game, I climbed up a large magnolia tree in my neighbor's yard and I disappeared into the foliage. A magnolia tree is a fortress. Their leaves are so dense that grass does not grow underneath them. For me, that tree became a refuge. It was the place to which I always ran, and I never lost another game of hide-and-seek. I loved sitting among the branches and watching the chaos of the game unfold around me. Unlike most of the kids, I didn't like the savagery of the chase, I just wanted to be safe. I found peace when I found a place to hide.

But hiding is harder than it sounds. The act of hiding requires that we admit certain things about ourselves. We must acknowledge that the threat is stronger than we are. When I played hide-and-seek, I had to admit that I wasn't the fastest kid in the neighborhood and that I was afraid of getting tackled. Standing in front of that magnolia tree, I had to admit that it could take better care of me than I could. I had to give up control. I had to trust the tree, certainly, but I also had to doubt myself. The prayers of Asaph that we explored in Chapter 5 are a full-scale rejection of any refuge we might find on our own. God doesn't care about our strength or our guilt, he just wants us to come and hide.

Pray Psalm 46 and admit your own fears. Pray it and let go of your own strength. Don't match your crisis strength-for-strength; match it with faith. Even the most powerful people in Scripture were better at hiding than they were at fighting. John was a "son of thunder," but pictured the saints crouching under the altar of God (Revelation 6:9–10). Peter was a rock, but he taught that salvation was guarded by God (1 Peter 1:5). Paul was a theological bully but coined the idea of our life being hidden in Christ (Colossians 3:3). Likewise, today's greatest Christian activists will be more effective if they hide better than they fight.

Pray Psalm 46 in weakness and let the power belong to God. Your body won't be whisked away to safety, but praying this psalm can help you live as if it is. The nations will keep raging and the kingdoms will totter, but that makes no difference to you. You are safe. You can face life's storm because your heart is nestled secure in the presence of God.

Let's pray.

Chapter 6

Prayers of Righteousness

Praying the Psalms alters the way we speak to God. The most notable change you might experience is when you pray the psalms of righteousness. These psalms don't just aspire to holiness, they declare it as an accomplished fact. Most of us feel comfortable asking God to *make* us righteous, as in Psalm 51:10, "Create in me a clean heart." In this kind of prayer, we come to God in all our unrighteousness, and ask to be transformed. The psalms of righteousness, however, are different. In them, we are forced to tell God how righteous we have already been. Consider these verses from Psalm 17:

> You have tried my heart, you have visited me by night,
> you have tested me, and you will find nothing;
> I have purposed that my mouth will not transgress.
> With regard to the works of man, by the word of your lips
> I have avoided the ways of the violent.
> My steps have held fast to your paths;
> my feet have not slipped. (vv. 3–5)

Saying such wonderful things about ourselves feels prideful, maybe even un-Christian, but plenty of psalms do this whether in whole or in part.

There is a good chance that most of these psalms originated from very particular situations, where the psalmist was right about something while the wicked were wrong. Even Psalm 17 appears to reference a specific moment where David could have joined with violent people but God's word steered him in the right direction. In that original context, these psalms make more sense. They rejoice that believers have stayed faithful, and they often ask for God's deliverance in return.

For us, however, these psalms are often less straightforward. We are thousands of years removed from the events that generated them. Praying through the Psalter means praying the psalms simply because they are there. Their original context isn't necessarily our context. In fact, depending on what we've been up to, we might be praying these psalms when we haven't been faithful at all. In our case, the psalms shape us more than they describe us. They help reframe our perspective and give us the chance to practice righteousness through prayer. They show us how to associate ourselves with God and claim his righteousness as our own. But that might be easier said than done.

Praying these prayers may be difficult because many of us have a complicated relationship with personal holiness. We have a hard time distinguishing between righteousness and *self*-righteousness, and we associate holiness with being judgmental or prudish. Righteousness is even leveraged as a weapon to fight political battles and push social agendas. Some churches teach that holiness is the primary message while others regard holiness with suspicion. So much of Scripture, from Old Testament to New, encourages believers to live holy lives, yet we have somehow turned this into a touchy subject.

The psalms of righteousness challenge this. They help re-center our understanding and balance our experience. They remind us that holiness is sacred, but only as it relates to our fellowship with God. These psalms are one of the great gifts of psalmic prayer because they dive headlong into a subject some of us have been avoiding, and they make holiness out to be as simple as it is good. In this chapter, therefore, we explore the theology and experience of praying the psalms of righteousness and consider some of the great treasures buried within.

The Battle between Good and Evil

From Genesis to Revelation, conflict is a mark of the redemption story. From the beginning, the Bible divides the world into two groups: the seed of the serpent and the seed of the woman. Hostility between the two is a defining reality for God's people until the very end. Jesus is the central figure in the struggle, but the conflict is a lens through which we can see the world. Most of the psalms were written in the midst of this conflict and psalmic spirituality is often drawn along combative lines.

As the conflict between good and evil rages, we have to pick our side. We must affiliate ourselves with one seed or another on a daily basis. The serpent, however, is craftier than any other creature (Genesis 3:1). He is always deceiving us and getting us to confuse right and wrong. We need decisive language embedded in our hearts. We need to practice allegiance so that aligning with God becomes an instinct. This can only be developed through repetition and that repetition can be found in the psalms of righteousness.

> My eyes are toward you, O God, my Lord;
> in you I seek refuge; leave me not defenseless!
> Keep me from the trap that they have laid for me
> and from the snares of evildoers! (Psalms 141:8–9)

We can see from Psalm 141 that God's people are good and his enemies are bad. There are no other categories. There is no room within these verses for people who belong to God but act like they don't. All of us have set traps for other people. We silently test the allegiance of friends or the performance of coworkers. We manipulate situations so that others fail and we succeed. We all do this, but the psalm acts like the only trap-setters are God's enemies. It assumes that the children of God are keeping their eyes on him. And if you pray this psalm, it all but forces you to identify with the righteous.

That is one of the great benefits of these psalms. They draw the lines for battle and then place us on the proper side. They do it for us, training us how to think before we ever leave our prayer closet. In Christ, God "delivered us from the domain of darkness and transferred us to the kingdom of his beloved Son" (Colossians 1:13). We are now, without question, on the side of God. In the words of Genesis 3, we *are* the seed of the woman. In the words of the Psalter, we *are* the righteous.

These psalms give us the opportunity to announce our allegiance to the Lord, something we probably need to say even more than God needs to hear. We practice that allegiance in prayer, reciting prayers that sound like marching orders. These psalms teach us to go to war.

> All nations surrounded me;
>   in the name of the Lord I cut them off!
> They surrounded me, surrounded me on every side;
>   in the name of the Lord I cut them off!
> They surrounded me like bees;
>   they went out like a fire among thorns;
>   in the name of the Lord I cut them off!
> I was pushed hard, so that I was falling,
>   but the Lord helped me. (Psalm 118:10–13)

This militant spirituality in the psalms of righteousness is overly simplistic, but incredibly helpful. There are numerous other psalms that reflect our complicated experience. Psalm 39, for instance, talks about a person who knows he is right but is having a hard time keeping his mouth shut because of it. Meanwhile, Psalm 60 is for anyone that can't seem to figure out if God is for us or against us. We can all relate to psalms like those because that's what life is like.

However, if the Psalter only described our spiritual confusion, then our spirituality would be marked by self-doubt. It's nice when the Psalter meets us where we are, but it's better when it orients us towards something more desirable. The psalms of righteousness do just that. They burst with a confidence that can only be found in the gospel experience.

Before I started praying the Psalms, my prayers were mostly announcements of my allegiance to old sin patterns. I would hem and haw with God, repeating to him how bad I was. Consequently, my spirituality was one of reluctance and hesitation. When I started praying these psalms, however, it changed how I saw the world and my place in it. The psalms of righteousness jam our flag into the ground and tell God that we are on his side. We declare that the gospel has worked and that we have been transferred from one kingdom to another. God has given us these prayers to recite gospel truths. Praying these psalms helps us rehearse our loyalty to him.

The Perfect Prayer

Allegiance, however, is just the beginning of what these psalms can provide. As I teach fellow believers to pray the Psalms, one of my favorite moments is when we get to pray Psalm 26 together. Before they have seen the psalm, I remind them of the ground rules of psalmic prayer. God put Psalm 26 in the Bible, so it is good for us to pray it. In addition, these words can shape our experience rather than simply describe it. One writer says that psalmic prayer gives us the chance to deliberately reconfigure our heart's syntax to mesh with the psalm's syntax.[17] In other words, we enter the psalm's spiritual environment instead of standing at the window and looking in.

After that introduction, we open our Psalter to pray one of the hardest psalms in the Bible. I challenge you to pray it now:

> Vindicate me, O LORD,
>   for I have walked in my integrity,
>   and I have trusted in the Lord without wavering.
> Prove me, O LORD, and try me;
>   test my heart and my mind.
> For your steadfast love is before my eyes,
>   and I walk in your faithfulness.
>
> I do not sit with men of falsehood,
>   nor do I consort with hypocrites.
> I hate the assembly of evildoers,
>   and I will not sit with the wicked.
>
> I wash my hands in innocence
>   and go around your altar, O LORD,
> proclaiming thanksgiving aloud,
>   and telling all your wondrous deeds.
>
> O LORD, I love the habitation of your house
>   and the place where your glory dwells.
> Do not sweep my soul away with sinners,
>   nor my life with bloodthirsty men,

in whose hands are evil devices,
  and whose right hands are full of bribes.

But as for me, I shall walk in my integrity;
  redeem me, and be gracious to me.
My foot stands on level ground;
  in the great assembly I will bless the LORD. (Psalm 26)

It makes sense to be startled by the perfection of this psalm, but praying it is an important part of our spiritual development. There isn't much about Psalm 26 that matches the human experience. We are too sinful for its descriptions. The psalm proclaims that we have rejected falsehood, but too often we eat of its delicacies (Psalm 141:4). Through the psalm we tell God that we have denounced hypocrisy but, just as badly as anyone, we cultivate evil and struggle to maintain integrity. Put simply, there is ample evidence why Psalm 26 should *not* be our psalm, and there is a good bit of theology to support our discomfort.

Whether we call it the flesh, the old self, or our sinful nature, there is an aspect of the human heart that rebels against God until the day we die. Even though God changes us, this sinful part remains as sinful as ever. It is virtually untouched by spiritual transformation. Of course, we know this from experience. We can work a long time to get victory over a particular sin, only to fall back into it in an instant. This is because our flesh was still lurking, waiting for its opportunity. While we were walking with God in the Spirit, our flesh kept the fires of rebellion still burning. This is why

Scripture speaks of salvation in terms of a war with our flesh. We fight it, even kill it, because it will never cooperate with our pursuit of God (Galatians 5:17; 1 Peter 2:11; Romans 8:13; Galatians 5:24).

Part of the fight we have against the flesh is our struggle not to be defined by it. There is only one person who lived the kind of life that is described in Psalm 26, and that was Jesus Christ. While every psalm points to him in one way or another, the psalms of righteousness draw a direct line. Jesus embodied them from beginning to end. He fulfilled the law that these psalms celebrate and personified the alliance that they proclaim. If we *study* these psalms, we learn about Christ's perfection and worship him as the Holy One of God. But, as we *pray* them, we are invited to experience his righteousness and be defined by his perfection.

Throughout the New Testament, we are taught to locate our identity in Christ, which is quite different from the identity we have in our flesh. The record of debt that stood against our flesh has been canceled so that we are free to experience life with God (Colossians 2:14, Romans 7:6). In fact, Jesus took our sin upon himself so that "we might become the righteousness of God" (2 Corinthians 5:21). The righteous requirement of the law has actually been fulfilled in us, so that we are now holy before the Lord (Romans 8:4). Believers have been so utterly transformed that we are called a new creation (2 Corinthians 5:17).

We Christians, therefore, live a double life. On the one hand, we are rebellious, while on the other, we are righteous. The believer is both a sinner and a saint. These are two concurrent truths, and we are constantly choosing to live according to one or the other. Because of our flesh, we will never have the kind of holiness that Psalm 26 describes. The question is not whether we are perfect enough to pray it, but whether we are willing to receive the identity of the One who could. This is the great challenge of Psalm 26: accepting the righteousness of Christ. It is the challenge of forgetting ourselves.

Some of us are so haunted by the flesh that we can hardly see past its pollution. Shame, failure, and brokenness can read like an epithet across our soul. Psalm 26 can seem almost un-pray-able. That is why Paul is always reminding Christians to disassociate themselves from the flesh and associate themselves with Christ. We have to forget what is behind, take off what is old, no longer consider the flesh, and set our minds on things above. It is one thing to believe that we are righteous in Christ, but it is quite another to pray like we are.

As I've prayed Psalm 26 with fellow believers, I've watched some of them physically squirm under the weight of its perfection. On more than one occasion, I've even seen Christians flatly refuse to pray it. It's just that hard. Yet that's precisely why it's so important. We have to decide what our identity is. As we have already mentioned, the psalms of righteousness announce our allegiance to God. Incredibly, however, they also help subvert the identity that accompanies our sin. One of the ways we nourish our flesh is to fixate on it. Yet we are free to embrace a different reality. Putting off one identity and putting on another is a key component to spiritual formation. This is how psalmic prayer reconfigures our hearts to match psalmic truths.

The Righteousness of Christ

Occasionally I catch myself praying without even realizing it. That may sound holy, but it really isn't. These aren't really prayers as much as they are self-flagellation. I catch myself asking God to make me new because I feel polluted. I consistently ask God to forgive me for sins I confessed long-ago because I still feel guilty. These mindless prayers are really just me asking God to give me something he already gave me. I keep asking because I keep feeling like I don't have it. When I catch myself doing this, I stop the "prayer" midcourse. I start thanking God that I'm new and forgiven. I start identifying myself with Jesus instead of my own flesh. I start praying prayers based on faith rather than prayers based on my feelings.

So many of us keep watch of our feelings and read them as if they were a spiritual thermometer. We let our sense of identity ebb and flow with however our thermometer reads.[18] But, in the psalms of righteousness, we are redirected to Jesus. Indeed we bask in him. Those psalms grab us by the scruff of the neck and force us to accept Christ's righteousness as our own. Praying these prayers means that we check Jesus's spiritual temperature and attach our personal identity to how *his* thermometer reads.

How does it feel to be Jesus right now? He is loved by the Father and is secure in his presence. He has done exactly what he was supposed to do. The Father looks at him and smiles. His enemies on earth still rage but he is certain of his victory over them. In other words, Jesus's spiritual temperature is amazing, which is how our spiritual thermometer should read. We should wake up in the morning and take Jesus's temperature instead of our own. We should hold loosely to our sin and failure and hold tightly to Christ's life and his experience.

As Christians, we believe that when God the Father looks at us, he sees the works of his Son. That is what it means to be clothed in the righteousness of Christ. It's time that we Christians look in the mirror and see the very same thing. It is time that we look at ourselves and see Jesus.

Imagine being at the right hand of God the Father this very minute. Imagine knowing that God is well-pleased with you. Imagine the freedom that God the Son has with God the Father, and the easy rapport between them. That is the spiritual environment of these psalms. Such things are not left to our imagination, because God wanted us to pray through the kind of experience that only Jesus is actually having.

The Lord dealt with me according to my righteousness;
    according to the cleanness of my hands he rewarded me.
For I have kept the ways of the Lord,
    and have not wickedly departed from my God.
For all his rules were before me,
    and his statutes I did not put away from me.
I was blameless before him,
    and I kept myself from my guilt.

> So the Lord has rewarded me according to my righteousness,
> according to the cleanness of my hands in his sight.
> (Psalm 18:20–24)

Some Christians may find it almost impossible to take their eyes off how they feel. Or maybe they find it suffocating to be so close to the righteousness of Christ. For such believers, these psalms are medicine for the soul. Keep reciting them until you believe them. Use the psalms of righteousness to practice the gospel experience of letting go of the flesh and accepting the identity of Christ. Quit obsessing about your own experience in sin and start obsessing about Christ's experience right next to the Father. We shouldn't wait until we feel as righteous as Jesus because we never will. We are, however, told to believe it. It is an act of sheer faith, and faith is a decision.

The Righteous Effects of Jesus

This reorientation around the righteousness of Christ has practical effects in the Christian life. It transforms the way we relate to fellow believers, especially for those of us who preach and give counsel. In the work of ministry, it is very easy to evaluate people according to the sinfulness of their flesh. These psalms, however, have convinced me that I need to be better at teaching people how to take the temperature of Christ, and how to appropriate that into their lives through the Spirit. That includes dealing with the reality of sin, of course, but Christian ministry should not point people towards the flesh. We should reflect Paul's letters instead, lifting believers to bask in the righteousness of Christ. We need to point people outside themselves rather than constantly having them take stock of their inabilities.

Secondly, this reorientation towards righteousness is a surprisingly powerful antidote against sin. I've spent many years trying to confess my way out of old sin patterns, mostly with limited results. But turning my attention away from those worthless things has helped me see beyond the sin-induced cycle. We shouldn't give up confessing sin, but I find it telling that there are about as many psalms that teach us how to proclaim our righteousness as there are ones that teach us how to confess our sin. When my spirituality started to reflect that balance, I found it easier to tell my flesh no. In fact, nothing makes you want to be holy more than recounting your holiness to God!

Likewise, there is a strange thing that happens as we pray psalms like Psalm 26. It forces us to pray in faith, saying things that only our Lord could say. We also mostly pray it out of obedience because none of us would normally say such things to God. Think about that for a moment. Doing something out of faith and obedience sounds just like the person in Psalm 26. We get there indirectly, but Psalm 26 has the uncanny ability to create the kind of person it describes! As the psalm describes Jesus, praying it actually helps us look like him. Psalm 26 sets the bar so high that we are essentially bullied into a surprisingly pure faith.

These psalms are indispensable to the Christian experience. They help us realize that we are not sneaking into the kingdom of

God. We belong there. Rebellion is not our narrative. Our position with the Father is as secure as Christ's. Because we are in Christ, we actually deserve to be with God. This is the gospel experience. It is the experience that we rehearse as we pray these psalms. According to Ephesians 2, we are seated with Christ in the heavenly places. Praying the psalms of righteousness will help you enjoy the view.

Reflection 6: Holiness and Communion

Praying Psalm 15

The book of Numbers reads like a comedy of errors. It can actually be organized by the different times when the people rebelled and God responded by killing them in various, unnatural ways. Looking back on the wilderness experience, the psalmist blithely describes the turbulent dance, "When he killed them, they sought him" (Psalm 78:34). Time after time, the people sinned, a large number were killed, and those who didn't die did better for a time. But that is not all that happened. Most of these cycles in the book of Numbers are punctuated by explanations of God's law. We might read these law sections thinking that God was bewildered by their sin, but I like to think that reiterating the law was God's way of assuring his children that he was still there. The law reminded them that they had not outrun his grace, and that their pollution had not polluted the purity of God.

For the people of the Old Testament, God's law was a delight. The law meant that God loved the Israelites enough to have a relationship with them, that he wanted to share his holy character with them. The law was God's holiness writ large. Through it, the Lord stepped out from the darkness of the holy of holies and took part in the rhythms of daily life. For this reason, receiving the law was a cause for celebration. It meant God was forging a relationship with people that didn't deserve it. Moses proclaimed the greatness of God's law as he delivered the Ten Commandments in Deuteronomy, saying that God's law meant God's nearness (Deuteronomy 4:7–8). It's a sentiment recounted in Psalm 147.

> He has not dealt thus with any other nation;
> they do not know his rules.
> Praise the LORD! (v. 20)

As Christians, we enter into fellowship with God without having to go through the gatekeeper of God's law. When God sent his Son, he manifested himself apart from the law and we, because of his Son, are justified without having to be obedient to it (Romans 3:21–28). Add to this that the Holy Spirit has put the law inside of us, and it's easy to understand why we have such a tricky relationship with the law. But the Psalms don't. They rejoice in God's law and encourage us to do the same. Praying the Psalms will mean that we praise God for giving the law, glorify him through it, and ask to be near it. Therefore, I would like to use this reflection to remind us of just how good it is that God shared his law.

I am here referring to only one particular part of God's law. I am not talking about the sacrificial laws of Leviticus or the civil laws that governed Israel's nation, because Jesus changed our relationship to both of those. He built a new community, the church, which put an end to the civil laws, and his sacrifice on the cross ended our need for the blood of bulls and goats. What we celebrate in psalmic prayer is God sharing his moral perfection with us through the law that still stands. It is the law contained in the Ten Commandments, what the theologians call the moral law of the Old Testament.

When we think of the law, we probably think about the perfection of God. We also might think that it is a standard of moral perfection by which we are judged. In our litigious culture, our minds teem with concepts like judges and prosecutors, defendants and attorneys. We think of evidence, guilt, acquittal, and verdicts. This courtroom imagery isn't foreign to the Bible, but it certainly isn't the whole story. Moses was excited to announce God's law because God was coming near. In fact, his personhood saturates his law. God's law is perfect because God is perfect. It revives the soul because God gives life. His law makes us wise because God shares what he knows. It causes us to rejoice because a God that gives law is a God that cares (Psalm 19:7–8).

There is reason to celebrate alongside the Psalter. When we pray the Psalms and come to a section that praises his law, we don't need to hesitate. We have the same God who shared his same holiness, and we can revel in those laws even though we aren't saved by them. In fact, not being saved by them frees us to delight in them. No one was ever saved by the law. From Old Testament saints to New Testament believers, Jesus is the only way of salvation. The celebratory spirit of the Psalter is not one of salvation accomplished by works, but a celebration of a God who loves, who speaks, and who wants to be involved in our lives. With that in mind, take a moment to pray this section of Psalm 119 and join in the ancient revelry.

> The LORD is my portion;
>   I promise to keep your words.
> I entreat your favor with all my heart;
>   be gracious to me according to your promise.
> When I think on my ways,
>   I turn my feet to your testimonies;
> I hasten and do not delay
>   to keep your commandments.
> Though the cords of the wicked ensnare me,
>   I do not forget your law.
> At midnight I rise to praise you,
>   because of your righteous rules.
> I am a companion of all who fear you,
>   of those who keep your precepts.
> The earth, O LORD, is full of your steadfast love;
>   teach me your statutes! (vv. 57–64)

There is a prayer that was used by ancient Christians that surprises me every time I come across it. It asks God "that the whole day may be perfect, holy, peaceful, and sinless."[19] It is an audacious prayer, to be sure, but it's as strange as it is audacious. I think most modern Christians wouldn't dare ask that our day be perfect or sinless. I imagine that many believers would think of that as being too legalistic. But the ancient church, along with the Scriptures, embraced the goodness of God's law, while we tend to simply embrace the goodness of God's grace. Like we discussed in this chapter, we might be so used to thinking of ourselves as God's lowliest servants that we might not dare to try and be his star pupil. The Psalms, once again, will challenge this kind of thinking.

The righteous, says Psalm 92:13, "are planted in the house of the LORD; they flourish in the courts of our God." Obedience to God's law is a form of communion with him, where we experience the character that he has shared. We don't earn our place with him through our obedience, but our perception of him is tied to it. "Blessed are the pure in heart," says Jesus, "for they shall see God" (Matthew 5:8). Or, as the psalmist says,

> Who shall ascend the hill of the LORD?
> And who shall stand in his holy place?
> He who has clean hands and a pure heart. (Psalm 24:3–4a)

As you pray the Psalms, don't be afraid to embrace God's law. Don't worry about it being a different way of salvation because the Word that was expressed in the law is the Word that became flesh to save you. Instead, see the law of God as something you can enjoy. Through these prayers, admire the ethical beauty and perfection of the Godhead and even have the audacity to aspire to it. You won't obey perfectly, but you can obey. In fact, the law of God, which once was carved into stone, now courses through our veins.

With that in mind, I encourage you to pray the words of Psalm 15. It is a psalm that describes holiness with the stated goal of dwelling with God. Don't read through this as a list of things you can't do, rather pray through this psalm and let your will dissolve into God's. The Spirit is active in you, and it is already doing those things described in the psalm. Allow yourself the chance to be this person. Don't worry about whether you will obey God perfectly, because you won't. God has always given his law to people he didn't expect could keep it. The point is communion, not salvation. Be holy simply for the fact that your God is holy, and it is the greatest privilege that we can be like him (Leviticus 11:44; 1 Peter 1:16). Loving God, after all, means keeping his commandments (John 14:15; 2 John 1:6).

> O Lord, who shall sojourn in your tent?
>   Who shall dwell on your holy hill?
> He who walks blamelessly and does what is right
>   and speaks truth in his heart;
> who does not slander with his tongue
>   and does no evil to his neighbor,
>   nor takes up a reproach against his friend;
> in whose eyes a vile person is despised,
>   but who honors those who fear the Lord;
> who swears to his own hurt and does not change;
>   who does not put out his money at interest
>   and does not take a bribe against the innocent.
> He who does these things shall never be moved. (Psalm 15)

Chapter 7

Praying Against Evil

Anyone who reads the Psalms will notice that there are a lot of psalms that call down God's judgment on other people. As we try to make the Psalms our words to God, these angry psalms can be troubling to pray. While the psalms of righteousness may be tricky, figuring out how to pray these psalms of judgment is a more pressing matter, simply for the fact that they pervade the Psalter. If you are going to pray *any* psalms, much less all of them, you have to know what to do with all those prayers against wicked people.

I've mentioned before that Psalm 63 has been a lifelong favorite of mine. It was the first psalm I consistently prayed, decades before I discovered psalmic prayer. It expressed my longing for God and pointed me toward his nourishment in lean and lonely years. It showed me that wilderness rations were a feast when they came from the hand of our Lord. At the end of the psalm, however, it says:

But those who seek to destroy my life
  shall go down into the depths of the earth;
they shall be given over to the power of the sword;
  they shall be a portion for jackals. (vv. 9–10)

I just skipped those lines because I never knew what to make of them. I had to do the same with Psalm 104, another favorite. On countless backpacking trips, I munched my trail mix and considered how God brought forth the mountains and made nests for the birds. The rhythms of nature, says Psalm 104, are the rhythms of God. Then, without warning, I would get to 104:35 which says: "Let sinners be consumed from the earth!" It always brought a harsh end to those happy moments. Similarly, Psalm 139, one of the most intimate psalms, ends with:

Oh that you would slay the wicked, O God!
  O men of blood, depart from me!
They speak against you with malicious intent;
  your enemies take your name in vain.
Do I not hate those who hate you, O LORD?
  And do I not loathe those who rise up against you?
I hate them with complete hatred;
  I count them my enemies. (vv. 19–22)

In this chapter, we will grapple with the imprecatory psalms. The word *imprecatory* comes from the word *imprecation*, which is a curse spoken against another person. In the psalms of righteousness, we see God's children portrayed as holy, entitled to God's blessings and deliverance. The imprecatory psalms, on the other hand, condemn God's enemies with equal zeal, heaping on them the curses that their wickedness deserves. The combative spirituality we touched on in the last chapter lands with full force in these angry psalms.

Before we go any further, however, we need to address whether such psalms are appropriate to pray. They sound eerily similar to the current rhetoric that makes it so hard for some believers to identify with the body of Christ. We might wonder if these psalms have a place in our conflict-riddled society. Do combative Christians need more kindling than what pundits and social media provide? Must peaceful believers use the aggressive language they have worked so hard to avoid? How do the imprecatory psalms aid our spiritual development and further the kingdom? Shouldn't we just think about the things that are pure and lovely and commendable (Philippians 4:8)?

I believe we need the imprecatory psalms now more than ever. Our society is not the first to be ripped apart by conflict. These psalms have served generations of believers that had much bigger problems than ours. These prayers are the script for anyone who suffers injustice. They gave voice to Jews who watched the temple burn and Christians who suffered under Nero. They offered a vocabulary for Africans enslaved in America and Russians oppressed by Stalin. We didn't invent conflict and avoiding it won't make it disappear. The bewildering way many believers respond to current problems shows me that we haven't yet learned how to handle our emotions. If we are losing our minds while ignoring the Psalter, maybe embracing the Psalter will help!

Identifying Evil

God expects us to pray against evil, and the Psalter sees evil everywhere. From foreigners marching on Jerusalem to fellow Israelites acting corruptly, wicked people are a never-ending source of affliction. Imprecatory psalms teach us to voice that affliction and pray against its source whenever and wherever we see it. When we pray in our own words, we likely pray "balanced" prayers where we weigh the good and bad of other people and try to be objective about our situation. Imprecatory psalms do no such thing. They attack. They have no regard for balance, and they teach us to quit playing it safe with God.

As you seek to identify the evil that surrounds you, Psalm 10 may help. According to the psalm, the wicked

> sits in ambush in the villages;
>   in hiding places he murders the innocent.
> His eyes stealthily watch for the helpless;
>   he lurks in ambush like a lion in his thicket;
> he lurks that he may seize the poor;
>   he seizes the poor when he draws him into his net.
> The helpless are crushed, sink down,
>   and fall by his might.
> He says in his heart, "God has forgotten,
>   he has hidden his face, he will never see it." (vv. 8–11)

Who (and what) does this in your world? Use the imprecatory psalms to pray against them (or that). It doesn't matter if you know them or if they are in your political party. It doesn't matter if they also do good things or if you want them to become a Christian. Other psalms pray through other experiences, but imprecatory psalms equip us for the battle.

As we take the offensive in prayer, we target three key sources of evil in the world: the devil, the ungodly, and our own sinful flesh. When we pray the imprecatory psalms, we pray against one or more of these evils. We can even pray the same psalm against different forms of evil each time. God wants us to join the fight, so let's consider how.

Praying Against the Devil

Scripture doesn't teach a lot about the devil, but we know him to be a personal agent of evil who strives to thwart the work of God. He, and the hosts who follow him, are constant advocates of evil. In our modern age, it may feel silly to admit that we believe in a devil, but humanity alone could not create all the atrocities we see in this world. There is an evil being who transcends us, and he wants death, destruction, and deception to reign.

What's surprising is how God has weaponized believers to bring about Satan's demise. In Luke 10, Jesus sent his followers ahead of him to prepare certain towns for his arrival. They preached and healed, lingering in places that were hospitable. During the ministry of these believers, Jesus saw the devil fall like lightning (Luke

10:1–20, especially 10:18). Later, John's Apocalypse ties Satan's defeat to the witness and martyrdom of the saints (Revelation 12:11). The message seems clear: we participate in God's divine battle with the devil. As the devil governs the principalities of this earth, Christians infiltrate and subdue the effects of his dominion.

That enemy, however, is not flesh and blood. We can't just go to a specific location to fight him face-to-face and, even if we could, we would be completely outmatched. In Eden, Eve was in trouble the very instant she started talking to the serpent. His power to deceive exceeds our power to discern. Similarly, looking ahead to Revelation, the serpent is depicted as a dragon with great civilizations in his grip. Our work, therefore, is prayer (Ephesians 6:12). God has ultimate power over the devil, we do not. God orders and allows worldly and spiritual events, so we direct our prayers to him. In one of the strangest passages of the New Testament, Jude reminds us not to pronounce judgments directly at the devil, saying that even the archangel Michael refrained from such audacity (Jude 1:9).

Even now, the devil and his agents are attacking believers and scheming to destroy the church. They are deceiving non-believers, trapping people in sin, and blinding our leaders to the truth. Yet this enemy has already been conquered, which is why prayer is so important. We pray to the Lord of the harvest to turn people's hearts, and we pray that God's kingdom will come on earth. Through imprecatory psalms we pray that the devil would be silenced, bound, and destroyed. We might pray something like this from Psalm 58.

[The devil has] venom like the venom of a serpent,
like the deaf adder that stops its ear,
so that it does not hear the voice of charmers
or of the cunning enchanter.
O God, break the teeth in their mouths;
tear out the fangs of the young lions, O LORD! (vv. 4–6)

Praying Against the Ungodly

A second way to use these psalms is to pray them against the ungodly. In a collective sense, these are the power-brokers and culture-makers that work against God's authority. Psalm 2 tells us that these powers want to burst the bonds of God's reign and cast away his authority (Psalm 2:3). We live with constant reminders that those who should embody God's justice do the opposite. They celebrate wickedness and "frame injustice by statute" (Psalm 94:20). The Psalter offers prayers against this kind of evil. We can use them wherever we see oppression, injustice, persecution of believers, or whatever seems out of alignment with the coming of God's kingdom.

There is an individual aspect to this as well. Time and again, the Psalter identifies individuals as a source of injustice in the world, and Psalms ask God to hold such people accountable. It doesn't matter whether you see these people in national headlines or in your neighborhood, there are ungodly people that hurt others, create conflict, and otherwise oppose God's justice. You can certainly pray for their salvation, but the imprecatory psalms give us permission and the vocabulary to pray boldly against their harmful behavior.

We may feel a bit shy on this point, but we should trust the Psalms more than ourselves. We are not called to judge the world, and that means neither condemning nor pardoning it. These are prayers, not public denunciations, and we are directed throughout the Psalter to pray this way. The world would be a better place if we learned how to pray hostile prayers and have measured public discourse. Too often we do the opposite, praying measured prayers and publicly acting with hostility toward others.

When it comes to hostile prayers, none matches the intensity of Psalm 109. Praying this psalm against someone is almost scary. But it reminds us that wickedness must be stopped, and that God is the one who will stop it. So we pray against people who act wickedly.

> He loved to curse; let curses come upon him!
> He did not delight in blessing; may it be far from him!
> He clothed himself with cursing as his coat;
> may it soak into his body like water,
> like oil into his bones! (vv. 17–18)

Praying Against Our Flesh

Evil doesn't just exist within the realm of spiritual principalities or the works of ungodly people; it dwells within our hearts as well. As we discussed in the previous chapter, our flesh is a willing participant in the evil that plagues this world. In the days of 1 Peter, believers were being ostracized in new and alarming ways. More and more, they were feeling the social cost of faith in Jesus. Yet, when Peter described their war against evil, he didn't marshal the church against worldly powers. Instead, he spoke of the war that raged inside the believer's soul (1 Peter 2:11).

Imprecatory psalms are invaluable in our war against the flesh. Christians typically don't want to sin, yet we struggle to pray aggressively against the cause of our sin. When we pray imprecatory psalms against our flesh, we see our sinful tendencies for what they are: insidious impulses that turn us away from God. We learn to hate our flesh, to condemn it, and call down God's judgment to silence it.

Paul says that when we sin, it is no longer we who sin but the sin dwelling in us (Romans 7:17). If we are in Christ then our flesh is a trespasser, polluting holy ground. And we need to attack. Watch how praying Psalm 64 against our flesh distances us from our sinful tendencies and reaffirms our alliance with God:

> Hide me from the secret plots of [of my flesh],
>   from the throng of evildoers [inside my heart],
> who whet their tongues like swords,
>   who aim bitter words like arrows,
> shooting from ambush at [me],
>   shooting at [me] suddenly and without fear …
>
> But God shoots his arrow at [my flesh];
>   [it will be] wounded suddenly. (vv. 2–4, 7)

I tend towards self-loathing, and it is easy for me to hate certain things about myself. I usually hate how I'm not bold enough and always have recurring, hateful thoughts about how I embarrassed myself all the way back in high school. I even replay long-ago confessed sins and hate myself for committing them. It's interesting how often we hate ourselves for things we've confessed but how rarely we hate the sin that we most need to fight. That's because our flesh controls these emotions. Self-loathing is just a smokescreen to keep us from hating the problematic evil that lurks behind the hate. But praying these psalms against our flesh can turn the table. We become the attacker instead of the attacked. We start hating the evil within our hearts instead of the silly things we can't change. It's liberating.

The Imprecatory Psalms and Intercessory Prayer

One of the more surprising things about the Psalter is how it spends hardly any time praying for other people. This is surprising because many of us can hardly think of prayer without thinking of intercession. As we have mentioned, we have sometimes reduced prayer to nothing other than intercessory prayer and that is something the Psalter will help change. At the same time, praying for others is a critical part of our war against evil. And as we intercede for the church and the world, the Psalter can be as helpful as it is with any other form of prayer.

When it comes to using the Psalter as intercession, I typically pray a psalm for someone when that psalm reminds me of them.

If I find that I'm neglecting someone, I just pray for them between psalms. That has been my usual way. But when I moved to a new pastorate, I faced the awkward task of praying for a congregation that I didn't really know. So, for the first few months, I decided to simply pray through the whole Psalter while I interceded for my new church family.

I was amazed at the result. Casting my church as the Psalter's main character allowed me to praise God for the good times they experienced and the hard times they'd endured. I told God about how the devil was hunting down this little church and I pleaded with him to vindicate the congregation in the eyes of the world. Psalmic prayer placed the local church in the cosmic struggle between light and dark, which is exactly where it belongs. It galvanized my prayers for my new church, perhaps even more than for my previous one, simply because familiarity with my prior congregation led me to pray for them in my own words. And our own words are never better than God's.

Praying imprecatory psalms for our friends and family, however, can feel out of place. I assure you it isn't. People often come to their pastor burdened by what is happening to their friends and family. Their loved ones are being blinded or oppressed, destroying themselves or hurting others. When evil is stirring, even close to home, we are called to act. We need to fight with the strongest weapons available and the most powerful weapon may just be the imprecatory psalms. I have sat with parents who prayed imprecatory psalms against the flesh of their child, and with a wife as she prayed against the flesh of her husband. Here is an example of how to do this (using a *son*, since I don't have one of those).

> Make haste, O God, to deliver [my son]!
> O LORD, make haste to help [him]!
> Let [his flesh] be put to shame and confusion
> [for it seeks his] life!
> Let [his flesh] be turned back and brought to dishonor
> [for it] delights in [his] hurt! (Psalms 70:1–2)

We often have a front row seat to what the flesh is doing to those we love, so we pray these prayers out of compassion rather than anger. I've even seen a husband pray an imprecatory psalm against his wife and it helped restore compassion for her that he had lost. We can't sit on the fence when sin plagues our brothers and sisters in Christ. They need more powerful prayers than we might pray on our own. They need us to take up arms on their behalf to help them find victory over the darkness.

The Imprecatory Psalms and the Gospel Experience

When Jesus tells us to love our enemies and pray for those who persecute us, we may wonder whether praying curses upon others is appropriate (Matthew 5:44). In other words, are these psalms congruent with the New Testament command to love our enemies? Also, when the gospel teaches that we are as guilty as anyone, is it right to throw imprecatory stones?

Jesus's command to love our enemies is not only compatible with the imprecatory psalms, they make them all the more necessary. These psalms have the unique ability to unburden our hearts from the grudges and resentment that makes loving others so difficult. As an example, we need only to look at the author of many of these fiery psalms.

David exemplified the harmony between love and imprecatory prayers. By comparing his prayers to real-world events, we see how his prayers freed him from bitterness and control. For instance, Psalm 59 describes a scene where wicked men prowl like wild dogs hunting for food. Whenever I pray Psalm 59, I have to spiritualize the threat, but it was David's real-world experience. Those dogs were bloodthirsty men, and the food they hunted was David. When he had the chance to speak to God about them, he vented his anger freely.

> For the sin of their mouths, the words of their lips,
>   let them be trapped in their pride.
> For the cursing and lies that they utter,
>   consume them in wrath;
>   consume them till they are no more. (vv. 12–13a)

David asked God to publicly expose these wicked men so everyone would see their failure (Psalm 59:11). He even comforted himself with the idea of looking at these enemies in triumph (Psalm 59:10).

Psalm 59 describes the time Saul sent men to find David so Saul could kill him (1 Samuel 19:11). David's friends had to smuggle him from person to person just to keep him alive. These men were as evil in real life as they appear in the psalm, yet David had a different attitude in real life than he does in the psalm. David gloated over his enemies in prayer but felt pangs of guilt for taunting Saul in real life (1 Samuel 24:5). Moreover, David asked God to consume these men, but he spared Saul's life in the cave (1 Samuel 24:7).

David's deep respect for Saul didn't keep him from praying aggressively against him and his men. Instead, imprecatory prayers gave direction to his angry thoughts. They enabled David to honestly name the evil and entrust himself to the justice of God. Anger only becomes sinful when we let it poison our hearts or we act on it against others. David did neither because David prayed. He spoke his mind in prayer so he could return to life as God's child and Saul's embattled servant.

David articulated this perfectly while speaking to Saul at the end of the cave incident: "May the LORD judge between me and you, may the LORD avenge me against you, but my hand shall not be against you" (1 Samuel 24:13). David didn't have to judge because David prayed. He entrusted himself to the judge and contented himself with whatever vengeance God deemed appropriate. Praying imprecatory psalms took all of this out of David's hands, and it can do the same for us. David loved his enemies even though he cursed them in prayer. Or, perhaps, David was able to love his enemies because he first cursed them in prayer.

Even more striking is Psalm 63, where David prayed that his enemies would go down to the pit. He even fantasized that his enemies would be killed by the sword and their bodies would be eaten by jackals (Psalm 63:9–10). The target for these prayers? Not Saul, but David's own son Absalom! David loved his son, but that love didn't keep him from praying vigorously against him. While he spoke these hot-tempered things to God, David commanded his men to "deal gently" with Absalom (2 Samuel 18:5).

Those lines from Psalm 63 may be the most extraordinary combination of faith and intimacy in all the Bible. David trusted God so much that he could ask God to do something that he actually didn't want. David didn't seek balance in his prayer, weighing the sin of Absalom against David's love for him. Instead, David confided in his Lord. He spoke the most unspeakable words to his God, knowing that prayer was the only place where he could share everything.

David's faith in God's justice meant that he could say anything to God and know that God would do what was good and just. He did not have to tell God what to do, he could simply open his heart to God. Some of the imprecatory psalms may seem like overreactions, but David was free to overreact in prayer because he knew God wouldn't overreact in real life. That is the epitome of a safe space.

These psalms free us by giving us the chance to experience God's acceptance at the deepest level. No one would ever pray these prayers if they were trying to earn God's favor. Instead, we speak freely to him and are fully known. The imprecatory psalms coax the darkest emotions out of us and display them to God, yet we are welcomed into his presence exactly how we are. We have nothing to hide and there is nothing we can say that would change his love for us. That is why these imprecatory psalms can show us gospel truth in the deepest corners of our heart.

Imprecatory Psalms for Now

The evil that troubles our world is temporary. The woman's Seed has already crushed the seed of the serpent. Christ triumphed over the principalities of this world through his death and resurrection (Colossians 2:15). Yet, for now, war rages in Christ's absence. The book of Revelation describes evil, sin, rebellion, war, and persecution but then an end to all war. Revelation's final chapters describe peace and unhindered worship. In that day, our life with God and fellow believers will not be contaminated by sin.

The Psalter pictures much the same thing. Psalm after psalm wrestles with the evil of this world and its assault on the believing community. There are laments, betrayals, accusations, plagues, and storms. Yet the Psalter points beyond the evil that prowls about this world. The imprecatory psalms strike a note of optimism, because they work off the assumption that good triumphs over evil, that God is willing and powerful enough to judge this world. War ends in the final line of the final psalm: "Let everything that has breath praise the LORD" (Psalm 150:6).

There will come a day when everything and everyone will be a worshiper of God. In the meantime, we fight through prayer. Like the Israelites who rushed the battlefield after Goliath was slain or heavenly armies following Christ on his white horse, we participate in the victory that has been won by our King. We attack confidently. We keep praying these psalms until the day comes when prayers like these are no longer needed.

Reflection 7: The Enemy Within

Praying Psalm 55

Early in my journey of psalmic prayer I had the same question as any newcomer: what do we do with all the evil in the Psalms? Like everyone, I knew I could pray against the devil, but I wasn't sure who else. There are so many of these prayers in the Psalter and so much evil in our world. Surely we should do more than just pray against the devil. Then, the first time I prayed through Psalm 55, I discovered what it meant to pray against the enemy within. I'd like to share that story as it illustrates just how helpful these prayers can be.

I was in a particularly difficult season of anxiety when I first prayed Psalm 55, so the opening lines caught my attention: "I am restless in my complaint and I moan because of the noise of the enemy" (vv. 2b–3). Noise. I've always described my anxiety as noise. It's like a buzzing in my head. The words the psalmist used in those first few verses continued to connect with my experience: anguish, terrors of death, fear, trembling, and a horror that overwhelms. This is the newsfeed of an anxious mind. The fact that the noise and fear are in my head means there's nowhere to run. There isn't something I can do nor is there enough sleep that I can get. The anxiety will remain, regardless, and that is the lament of the psalm:

> I say, "Oh, that I had wings like a dove!
> I would fly away and be at rest;
> yes, I would wander far away;
> I would lodge in the wilderness;
> I would hurry to find a shelter
> from the raging wind and tempest." (vv. 6–8)

I still remember praying that psalm for the first time. I wasn't sure if we were supposed to put our emotional struggles into the Psalter, but it was too late. I was hooked. Psalm 55 was *my* psalm. I didn't care about its original context or its connection to the rest of Scripture. I wasn't even trying to figure out how Jesus fulfilled it. The most surprising person I saw in that psalm that day was me. These words were for me! I didn't have to study Psalm 55 to know it, because I could live alongside it. I could use it.

In Chapter 1, we looked at a quote from Athanasius, who encouraged ancient believers to use the Psalter for themselves. He said that we are observers of most of Scripture, but we are *users* when it comes to the Psalms. Throughout Scripture, God comes to us through his word and his Spirit, but through the words of the Psalter, we can go to God. They name our circumstances and pull us through the psalmic words into the presence of God. They bring us to his throne with our circumstances in tow. Psalm 55 allowed me to be anxious, but it also gave me some tools to confront my anxiety. As the rest of the psalm unfolds, we see the cause of David's affliction. Apparently, a close friend had betrayed him.

> For it is not an enemy who taunts me—
> then I could bear it;
> it is not an adversary who deals insolently with me—
> then I could hide from him.
> But it is you, a man, my equal,
> my companion, my familiar friend.
> We used to take sweet counsel together;
> within God's house we walked in the throng. (vv. 12–14)

Then later:

> My companion stretched out his hand against his friends;
> he violated his covenant.
> His speech was smooth as butter,
> yet war was in his heart;
> his words were softer than oil,
> yet they were drawn swords. (vv. 20–21)

I'm no psychologist, but I feel like that's what happens when I'm anxious. My "friend," my inner voice, turns on me. It's a voice that I mostly trust. It's the voice I use to preach the gospel to myself and it gives narrative shape to my life. It even makes funny little comments that keep me entertained through the monotony of life. Then, suddenly, that voice goes to war. It's as if all those smooth words were lulling me into thinking we were friends. It brings me close just to stab me with drawn swords.

This was the moment I fell in love with psalmic prayer. I first started praying the psalms as a spiritual experiment. I didn't know that it was a practice that was long used by ancient Christians, or that the church had largely forgotten it. I wasn't even sure anyone else ever prayed the Psalms. What I did know was that this psalm named something I couldn't. It identified an enemy that was so close to me that I couldn't recognize him. Of course, anxiety isn't necessarily sinful, but it mostly says sinful things, and I needed someone to tell me that. We need to listen to our anxiety to know why it is there, but we also need to learn how to ignore all of the bad things that it says. I needed someone to call my anxiety to account for the lies it proclaimed.

There isn't much of an assignment with this reflection, but I wanted to share my story in hopes that it could help you appreciate the intimacy of the war being waged. This war rages in our hearts with the same ferocity that it rages between heaven and hell. And hell doesn't fight fair. It uses our weaknesses and struggles against us, which makes the battlelines all the more confusing.

I haven't yet learned how to ignore the voice of fear, but that was never the point. David might have felt better after praying Psalm 55, or maybe he didn't. The Psalms are not medicine, they are prayers. They are prayers, composed in the tangled mess of this world, that bring us into the presence of God. The lesson that clinched my love of psalmic prayer was that God wanted to hear my struggle, even when it was raw and unruly; even when I was still being swallowed by it. Psalm 55 taught me how to go to war regardless of the enemy and regardless of whether I thought I could win.

Psalm 55 also alerted me to the danger of my inner voice. As a result of that psalm, I started trusting my inner monologue a bit less. I now know that a voice that speaks smooth words can also wield swords. Smooth words are easier to ignore than anxious ones. In fact, the psalms make it sound as though God's voice is the only voice we can trust, and that's not a bad way to live. As another psalm says, "the words of the LORD are pure words" (Psalm 12:6). They are the only words we can trust in this topsy-turvy world.

In Psalm 55, God says that he will not let the righteous be moved. Evil, not the righteous, will end up in the pit. The threats and accusations of our inner voice are the mouthpiece of an enemy within and, though his swords are sharp, his days are numbered. Christ is on his throne and God is keeping his children safe.

Chapter 8

The Silence of God

One of my worst spiritual droughts came during a ministry internship I did in my twenties. I probably went six months with no sense that God cared for me or heard me when I prayed. Strangely, this dry spell happened while my ministry was thriving. Every physical indicator said that all was well, but my heart was like an empty tomb. I didn't doubt the truth of God, just his love for me. But I kept going in ministry. I led Bible studies that talked about a God I wasn't experiencing. We studied God's promises, which felt like they were for everyone but me. It was miserable.

I was in a panic most of that time. I still remember walking to the church in the dead of night, alone, just to sit in the dark and cavernous sanctuary. I prayed and I waited. I heard nothing and sensed nothing. A church can be a creepy place at night, but I welcomed it; I wanted to feel something, anything. I desperately wanted to know what was wrong so I could fix it. In fact, not knowing why I felt so lost was almost as bad as the feeling of being lost.

Looking back on it now, I still don't know what was happening, which only confirms my suspicion that spiritual loneliness is part of our normal experience as Christians. We should expect the wilderness. That truth alone would have helped in my time of trial. I assumed the Christian life meant getting delivered from the wilderness, where Scripture makes clear that the life of faith often means walking right straight into it. Who needs faith on the mountaintop? We often forget that the still waters of Psalm 23 are accompanied by a trip through the valley of the shadow of death. Wilderness happens.

Throughout this book, we have talked about the experience of believing God's truth. For the most part, we have tried to show that what we feel should be determined by what we believe. But sometimes that doesn't work. Sometimes how we feel completely swallows us up to the point that we hardly know what to believe. In those moments, the Psalter takes our feelings seriously. We can use the Psalms when we feel broken and alone, knowing they won't just tell us to toughen up. In fact, the psalmist is more likely to confront God for his lack of action than to blame us for our lack of strength. The Psalms are for us to use, and God laid them like breadcrumbs to lead us through the dark and lonely wilderness.

The Silence of God

As we have seen in previous chapters, the Psalter pictures a world where we are completely dependent on God. It's a great way to live, of course, but it only makes spiritual darkness all the more alarming. Sometimes, God just stops speaking. He stops assuring us and stops giving spiritual nourishment. It is a source of confusion and fear among God's creatures: "You open your hand, [your creatures] are filled with good things. When you hide your face, they are dismayed" (Psalm 104:28b–29a).

Every generation of the church has examined this silence in their own way. The Westminster Confession of Faith offers one of my favorite discussions, wrestling with the subject in terms of assurance:

> The assurance true believers have of their salvation may be shaken, lessened, or interrupted for various reasons: from neglecting to preserve it; from committing some particular sin, which wounds the conscience and grieves the Spirit; from some sudden or strong temptation; or from God's withdrawing the sense of his presence and allowing them to walk in darkness. Nevertheless, they are never completely without God's seed, the life of faith, the love of Christ and of other believers, and the sincere heart and obedient conscience, out of which the Spirit may revive this assurance in due time and by which they are in the meantime kept from complete despair.[20]

The comfort of this teaching is that assurance is not an essential part of salvation. In other words, you can have salvation without having assurance. Many believers assume that *feeling* saved is the same as *being* saved, to the point of needing to be "re-saved" whenever their assurance falters. The Confession disagrees, as does the Psalter. The Psalms regularly describe the feeling of being alienated from God, but they rarely question the fact that we belong to him.

The Confession also teaches that our assurance can be shaken for a number of reasons. The one that stands out most is that God sometimes just lets his children walk in darkness. There may be nothing wrong. You may not have sinned or have an emotional disorder; you may just feel an inexplicable form of spiritual depression.[21] God did this with saints like Elijah, but it happens every day to normal believers. God sometimes lets us walk in darkness so that we will better appreciate his light. I'm glad the Confession has the theological grit to admit it. In other words, you will feel abandoned by God. It is as normal as feeling loved by him.

Some readers have experienced trauma that only makes their darkness darker. We cannot always fathom other people's pain, but we can take comfort knowing that there is no day too dark for the Psalter. Many of the Psalms were composed when every particle of light seemed to be draining from the world. For that reason, the Psalter accompanies us into our spiritual darkness, where only God can see a way through.

> If I say, "Surely the darkness shall cover me,
>   and the light about me be night,"
> even the darkness is not dark to you;
>   the night is bright as the day,
>   for darkness is as light with you. (Psalm 139:11–12)

Whether in times of spiritual or physical affliction, sin, or emotional distress, the Psalter validates our experience and walks alongside us. It speaks for us and to us, even when God doesn't seem to be talking.

In this chapter, then, we explore the silence of God. We will use the psalms of the Sons of Korah because they are a masterclass in this topic (Psalms 42–49, 84–85, 87–88). They are the most vibrant, poetic, and provocative psalms in the Bible. In particular, we will use Psalms 42–43. These two psalms were meant to be read together and we will treat them as a single unit. I will share my own interpretation of these psalms as they have guided me in prayer. Mine are not the comments of a biblical scholar but as someone who has experienced the Christian life through these psalms. I am not offering a definitive interpretation, but showing how these psalms can be a companion.

Naming the Silence

Psalm 42 begins with an image of a deer. It is a famous bit of imagery, but it's probably done as much to hinder our interpretation of the psalm as it has enhanced it. The deer is panting for flowing streams and most of us imagine him in a hardwood forest, perhaps Appalachia, surrounded by green trees and mossy rocks. If that were the case, things wouldn't be all that dire. The deer would be hoping for water, maybe after a hard day's journey. I think this image resonates with us because most of us sit in comfort and yearn for a luxuriant experience with God.

But the psalm is actually quite disturbing. Israel was more desert than forest. Imagine this deer standing in a dry riverbed, surrounded by scrub trees, with his knees shaking and belly swollen. The heat would be suffocating. The deer needs flowing streams because the few stagnant pools it can find are putrid. This is the place for a camel, not a deer. The deer is in the wrong place at the wrong time. The deer is dying.

Christian imagination often makes spiritual darkness more poetic than it really is. John of the Cross wrote a poem, *Dark Night of the Soul*, that romanticized his pain. His dark night was a lonely one that turned into a rendezvous with God. However unpleasant in the moment, the poem quickly whisks us to a fanciful end that gives us hope (and probably the expectation) that our pain will be as poetic as his. Christians have popularized the concept, wearing their "dark night of soul" like a badge of honor, hoping to emerge from it a poetic saint. In contrast, the Psalter never romanticizes suffering. God cares too much for the afflicted to make their pain inspirational.

Similar is the poem, "Footprints in the Sand." It imagines us looking back on a troubling time, only to find one set of footprints. God abandoned us and we walked alone, or so we thought. The poem assures us that we were never alone, that those were God's footprints, not ours. He was carrying us. It's comforting and not unbiblical. God does carry his children (Deuteronomy 1:31). Psalm 77, however, paints a darker picture. In the psalmic version, we look back and see only one set of footprints. Indeed, they are ours. God's footprints are the ones not seen (Psalm 77:19).

Sometimes we are alone and there is nothing inspirational about it. Sometimes God is leading us, but our own footprints are all we can see. Sometimes we are like that deer, struggling merely to hang on. There is no secret rendezvous with God and no lessons for observers to learn. In fact, if we are truly alone, there won't be anyone watching. Our only companion, says the psalmist, may be darkness itself (Psalm 88:18).

This is the isolation that the psalmist feels in Psalm 42. The person who wrote this psalm had been appointed a leader in Israel's worship (1 Chronicles 6:31–37). He would have been part of the religious festivals and possibly led the processions. He organized events and worked with his team to make things happen. If he did his job right, pilgrims had a good festival and worshipers were able to worship God. It was meaningful work but, for some reason, it had been taken away from him.

The psalmist could no longer attend or lead worship in the temple. In fact, he wasn't even in Jerusalem. According to Psalm 42:6, he was in "the land of Jordan," which probably meant that he was near the upper reaches of the Jordan River. Spiritually and geographically speaking, he was in the middle of nowhere, removed from every important aspect of Jewish spirituality. Being that far north meant that he was surrounded by people who were on the fringes of the Jewish religion. This was the region where Jeroboam set up a replica of Jerusalem's temple and it was seen as an abomination (1 Kings 12:29). We can hear the pain that his isolation caused:

These things I remember,
as I pour out my soul:
how I would go with the throng
and lead them in procession to the house of God
with glad shouts and songs of praise,
a multitude keeping festival. (Psalm 42:4)

In the time of Jesus, the Jews celebrated the Feast of Tabernacles in Jerusalem with dramatic processions. Every morning during the feast, a huge horn blew and a priest marched from the Temple Mount down to the Pool of Siloam. The priest drew out water and paraded it back up the hill.[22] A multitude of believers followed him, probably chanting psalms along the way. I wonder if this was the kind of scene the psalmist remembered.

Memory is an important part of our spiritual formation. Many psalms recite the personal memories of the psalmist or historical events in Israel's past. Memory matters because it is a standard by which we can judge the present. The psalmist had experienced good times with the Lord, and he wanted to get back to that. Other psalms recite how God had been good to their forefathers or how those same forefathers wandered into sin. When you learn to pray the Psalms, you may stumble your way through these historical retellings, but when it feels like God has stopped speaking, remembering God's works in the past may be all that you have to hang on to.

In Psalm 42, the psalmist mostly remembers what he has lost. His purpose and his identity had vanished. There were no religious processions in the north country, no temple feasts to lead. He could write the most beautiful psalm and there might never be anyone to hear it. Yet he would have known Psalm 139 and its lesson that we can never be separated from God. But his feelings and his theology were out of alignment. We hear him try to reconcile the two with a refrain that is repeated three times in Psalms 42–43:

> Why are you cast down, O my soul,
> and why are you in turmoil within me?
> Hope in God; for I shall again praise him,
> my salvation and my God. (Psalm 42:5)[23]

He shouldn't have been downcast, but he was. He should have been able to muster some hope, but he couldn't. The psalmist names his problem in the form of a question asked by others: "Where is your God?" (Psalm 42:3) If God were flexing his muscles and things were going as they should, non-believers could never ask this question. Only when God's people seem abandoned do they get to gloat like that. The problem with such a question is that it's contagious. We can only hear someone ask it for so long before we start asking it ourselves. *Where are you God? Am I alone?*

Interpreting the Silence

Early in Psalm 42, the psalmist seems confused, as his mind darts between his isolation, the cynics that mock him, and the God he longs to be near. When he asks, "Why are you downcast, O my soul?" it feels like an honest question. There is little sense of direction, but a deep sense of uncertainty. Yet things change in the second half of the psalm. He starts to figure out the source of his predicament and that sheds some light on his situation. It was God who did this:

> Deep calls to deep
> at the roar of your waterfalls;
> all your breakers and your waves
> have gone over me. (Psalm 42:7)

They were *God's* waterfalls, *God's* breakers, and *God's* waves. This is no small realization. He is having a hard time because God has laid a difficult burden on him. His situation wasn't caused by an enemy, the psalmist has figured out that God is the culprit. And this realization breathes optimism back into his heart. We can hear it as the psalm moves on:

> By day the LORD commands his steadfast love,
> and at night his song is with me,
> a prayer to the God of my life. (v. 8)

I often feel better about my situation when I know the cause of God's silence. Does this happen to you? Have you ever stumbled through a spiritual wilderness, then realized why you were in it? Doesn't that realization come with the expectation that things will get better, and get better soon? I do this all the time, and I think the psalmist does the same.

We can almost hear his sigh of relief, saying something like: "Okay, I get it. I'm stuck out here because God was teaching me a lesson. Let me just confess some sin or do a Bible study on God's discipline and I'll be done with this." What joy must have filled his heart when he imagined that his trial was nearly over. He could finally turn the page and move on. As the rest of the psalm unfolds, however, we quickly realize that his spiritual discovery failed to alleviate his pain.

> I say to God, my rock:
>   "Why have you forgotten me?
> Why do I go mourning
>   because of the oppression of the enemy?"
> As with a deadly wound in my bones,
>   my adversaries taunt me,
> while they say to me all the day long,
>   "Where is your God?" (vv. 9–10)

Wham! He falls right back in the pit.

God told Israel why they were in the wilderness at the *beginning* of their wilderness experience. They weren't in the wilderness to figure out why they were there, and they didn't get to leave it when they realized their sin. They had to stay there until every last one of them died. God usually has a different timetable than ours, which means figuring out our problem may do nothing to get us out of the pit. God won't necessarily begin speaking just because we realize why he was silent.

I know people who have barely set foot into a spiritual wilderness before they have a fully developed theory as to why God put them there. They know what lesson they need to learn and what it will take for them to learn it. They seem to know as much about the wilderness as God does! Yet, many of us are in that wilderness specifically because God is tired of us playing god. He wants to wrestle control away from our hands by placing us in the wilderness, but the wilderness just becomes another place where we obsess over having control.

As I walk with fellow believers through times of trial, we work to figure out why the trial is happening. I don't feel like I've done my job until they can discern what God is doing in their lives. However, I try to walk a fine line between being a good pastor and being one of Job's bad friends. His friends stood around and theorized when they should have kept their mouths shut. Unbeknownst to them, their theories put God in a box, in the middle of a book that proclaims God's freedom from boxes.

Our spiritual trials won't always make sense, but one lesson I know we should learn from them is that God is God. When we feel we are being stripped bare, it is okay not to know why. When God seems far away, it is okay to simply wait for him to return. We don't have to create a map and start planning our route. We can simply keep speaking to him and believe that we will be delivered.

Fighting the Silence

One thing that every psalmist does is fight. We have discussed this elsewhere, but the psalmist handles God's silence differently than we do today. The psalmist kicks and screams in the midst of hardship and rarely questions why the hardship is there. We typically do the opposite. We analyze what God is up to but then endure whatever comes our way like obedient church mice.

The flicker of life that we see in our psalmist comes in Psalm 43, when he starts to fight God. Up to this point, he had been a victim of isolation, an object of mocking, and the target of God's waves and breakers. Now he enters into the ring and starts throwing his own punches:

> Vindicate me, O God, and defend my cause
> against an ungodly people,
> from the deceitful and unjust man
> deliver me!
> For you are the God in whom I take refuge;
> why have you rejected me?
> Why do I go about mourning
> because of the oppression of the enemy?
>
> Send out your light and your truth;
> let them lead me;
> let them bring me to your holy hill
> and to your dwelling! (vv. 1–3)

The last thing we need to do when God is silent is stay silent in reply. God would rather we fight with him than hide. Psalm 43 is full of ill-tempered prayers, but they are prayers saturated with faith. "Vindicate me!" "Deliver me!" "Lead me!" The psalmist essentially tells God to do his job. He even takes a subtle dig at God in Psalm

43:2. He says that he has been seeking God as his refuge, which would imply that the psalmist is safe from enemy oppression. But is the psalmist safe? No, he goes about mourning because of it.

This touches on a surprising theme that permeates the Psalter. The Psalms regularly ask whether God is keeping his end of the bargain or not. Our world is broken and bad things happen to godly people. Whose fault is that? Things don't look like they should, but we humans can't make things right. What are we supposed to do about it?

We tend to be like Job's friends as we theorize about the silence of God. They saw their friend's plight and came up with any and every reason why it must be Job's fault rather than God's. They thought they were "protecting" God's character by laying the blame on Job, but they actually sound like the first humanists.

My favorite banjo player has a song called "Jonah & the Whale."[24] It has a line that has become a slogan for me when I pray. From the belly of the whale, Jonah cries out to God, "You're not the one whose hands are tied." That's what the psalmist is saying. It's what most every psalm is saying: "I'm not God, you are!" It's an insolent demand, but it's the admission of every prayer. Our hands are tied. God's are not. He should do something. He needs to do his job and keep his end of the bargain.

Of course, we are never keeping our end of the bargain, which only makes our theories about our failures all the more compelling. But God didn't just give us prayers that recount our own failures, he gave us prayers that insinuate his. What an incredible thought!

There are plenty of psalms that imply or outright accuse God of failing his people, and God lets those prayers be prayed. I think that's because God wants us to look at him even when we are the guilty party, something we discussed in Chapter 5. Jonah was the guilty party, but his hands were tied. He wasn't getting out of that fish by himself. Likewise, the psalmist can't make it back to God's holy hill on his own. God would have to bring him there. *You're not the one whose hands are tied.*

Spirituality and the Silence of God

Psalm 43 ends with the same question that has nagged him throughout:

> Why are you cast down, O my soul,
>   and why are you in turmoil within me?
> Hope in God; for I shall again praise him,
>   my salvation and my God. (v. 5)

With each passing refrain comes the realization that the psalmist's spiritual practice hasn't worked as he hoped. The psalmist named his problem, realized what was happening, and called God to action, but he still finds himself in the same existential space. He is still wondering why his soul is downcast. His heart remains in turmoil even though he's gone through the process that usually brought him relief. This brings us to a final, all-important point: spiritual practice doesn't always solve spiritual problems. Sometimes we go through our spiritual regimen and nothing changes.

God is a personal being and that comes with all the trials and tribulations of interacting with another person. We sometimes forget that. Instead, we approach Christian spirituality as if it were a vending machine. We think that prayer and Bible study should yield certain results. That isn't always the case. Spirituality can guide us through dark times, but it won't always resolve or prevent them. In fact, spirituality is less like a vending machine and more like those claw games where you can't quite grab the stuffed animal. We long for something that is impossible to possess, and we grab at things just beyond our reach.

Our God is a God who shrouds himself in darkness and speaks in an inaudible voice. He is the kind of God who best reveals his love when his children walk through the valley of the shadow of death. God is glorified in our search for him even more than our finding him. He is more interested in our spiritual fight than our spiritual victory. The apostle Paul, at the very end of his life, boasted that he had kept the faith (2 Timothy 4:7). He didn't boast that he had been to Spain or stood before Caesar. He didn't boast that he had started countless churches and written over half of the New Testament. He didn't even boast that he had transformed the social order of western civilization! He boasted that he still believed in Jesus, as if that was his greatest accomplishment. Maybe believing in God is harder than we make it out to be. Maybe we should give ourselves permission to struggle. Maybe we should expect the silence of God.

Reflection 8: Abandoned by God

Praying Psalm 44

As I mentioned before, the Sons of Korah wrote some of the boldest psalms in the Bible. None are more daring than Psalm 44. In this psalm, the psalmist accuses God of outright abandonment. Unlike the Psalms of Asaph, there is no lingering question as to whether Israel deserved God's judgment. In Psalm 44, the believer has done nothing wrong. If bad things are happening it is not because of judgment, but a dereliction of duty on the part of God. Or worse, God has simply ceased to be good.

The psalm begins with strong, confident statements about God's power to save. The opening lines celebrate God's wonders and how he drove out the nations to make Israel a home in the promised land. The Jewish forefathers were mere shepherds. They didn't drive out fierce nations with their own swords, but by the mighty hand of God (Psalm 44:1–3). After that, the psalmist recounts how God had been the savior of the current generation just like he was in generations past: "For not in my bow do I trust, nor can my sword save me" (v. 6).

These first eight verses of Psalm 44 picture a nation that was the creation of God. Whatever the people were, and wherever they lived, it was the result of God's power and his provision. These first eight verses are beautiful, but the psalm abruptly turns. The gloves come off:

> But you have rejected us and disgraced us
> and have not gone out with our armies.

You have made us turn back from the foe,
and those who hate us have gotten spoil.
You have made us like sheep for slaughter
and have scattered us among the nations. (vv. 9–11)

These are vicious accusations that play upon our greatest fears. The psalm describes a situation where God might just up and leave his children. In later verses, the psalmist makes it clear that this abandonment was no fault of their own.

All this has come upon us,
though we have not forgotten you,
and we have not been false to your covenant. (v. 17)

We often talk about "life verses" in Christian circles. These are Bible verses that hold some specific connection to us, and we make them into a kind of slogan. Like ancient Israelites writing the Shema on their doorposts, these verses are signposts for us. My life verse, the one I live by more than any other, is Exodus 14:11: "Is it because there are no graves in Egypt that you have taken us away to die in the wilderness?"

Sure, there are Bible verses that I aspire to, and plenty that speak to my heart of God's grace and love. But, if I am being honest, I am always quietly expecting that God will leave me. It is the fear of those Israelites in the wilderness, that the God who brought me this far will suddenly go no further. It is the fear that God will pull the rug out from under his children.

This is why Psalm 44 is so alarming to me. It is my worst fear realized. It makes it sound like God isn't as good as we thought he was, or that his promises might come to an end. Psalm 44 says that God sold his people but thought so little of them that he didn't even demand a high price! (Psalm 44:12) It claims that God turned his back when his people were doing good but would come banging down their door if they stretched out their hands to foreign gods. In other words, God only pays attention when he is counting our sins (Psalm 44:20–21).

The psalm even says this trouble has come upon them because they are being faithful to the Lord. In other words, they are sacrificing themselves for God, but he isn't lifting a finger for them: "Yet for your sake we are killed all the day long; we are regarded as sheep to be slaughtered" (v. 22).

This is a dreadful psalm, and if you have ever felt as desperate as this then you need a prayer like this. If you ever feel like you have done what you are supposed to do but God hasn't kept his end of the bargain, then turn to this psalm and lay your accusations before him. Maybe you have endured tragedy or been abused, and you tried to handle it like a good believer should, yet God just sat there, silent. This psalm is for anyone who feels like the greatest injustice they have endured comes from God and not from man.

This psalm gives us a chance to shake our fist at the Lord. It shows God's kindness that he lets his children speak this way, but it speaks to the brokenness of our Christian experience that we would ever need to. God doesn't always seem fair, or just, or good. God sometimes feels so negligent that we need words like those in Psalm 44:23, "Awake! Why are you sleeping, O Lord?" We are told elsewhere that our God never slumbers nor sleeps, but this psalm lets us know that we may still feel as if he does.

When Paul was writing his letter to the Romans, he wanted to express how secure our salvation is because of Jesus Christ. In Romans 8:35, he asks a rhetorical question: "Who will separate us from the love of Christ?" He continues by offering some situations we might think could separate us. "Shall tribulation, or distress, or persecution, or famine, or nakedness, or danger, or sword?" These are tragedies that could dislodge our grip on God, but Paul's point is that they will never dislodge God's grip on us.

Then Paul summarizes that list with an Old Testament quote. I imagine him thinking over the many chapters in the Old Testament, trying to find the worst-case scenario. Does the Old Testament ever make it sound like God would abandon his children? If he could find such a verse, then it would strengthen his argument. Not surprisingly, Paul lands on Psalm 44. In the most breathtaking section of Scripture, Paul inserts a quote from one of the darkest psalms in the Bible. He wants to prove that our darkest fear will never come true because our union with Christ secures us from every threat that could befall us. You don't need me to explain it further, just watch how Paul uses Psalm 44:22:

> Who shall separate us from the love of Christ? Shall tribulation, or distress, or persecution, or famine, or nakedness, or danger, or sword? As it is written,
>
> > "For your sake we are being killed all the day long;
> > we are regarded as sheep to be slaughtered."
>
> No, in all these things we are more than conquerors through him who loved us. For I am sure that neither death nor life, nor angels nor rulers, nor things present nor things to come, nor powers, nor height nor depth, nor anything else in all creation, will be able to separate us from the love of God in Christ Jesus our Lord. (Romans 8:35–39)

Paul's answer is *no*, God will never abandon us. Psalm 44 may feel true, but it will never be true. The only person that Psalm 44 describes is God's own Son, Jesus Christ. Just like Psalm 44:1–8, Jesus did everything by the power of God. Then, just like Psalm 44:9, God abandoned him to his enemies. God didn't protect him and didn't exercise divine power on his behalf. He sold his Son and demanded no high price. Psalm 44 should have been true for us because of our sin, but it was true of Jesus Christ instead. He was forsaken by God so that we never will be. Jesus took our place.

T*here are many* ways to pray the Psalms. The same psalm may even minister to you in different ways during different seasons of life. I encourage you now to pray Psalm 44 and use it for whatever purpose you need.

If you are feeling abandoned by God, use Psalm 44 to call him to account. There have been a couple of times that I used the words of this psalm to vent my anger at God. In those times, my heart was too raw to make it about Jesus. I needed the words to be about me because it described what I was already thinking. The psalm said things I'd be afraid to say on my own. If that is where you find yourself, then pray that way. Rage against the silence of God. The Lord would rather you doubt his love than isolate yourself in unbelief.

Other times we need to be reassured. Maybe we are more fearful than angry. Or maybe we don't feel like raging against the silence of God. Either way, we want to see Jesus and are ready to listen to the message of Romans 8. If that's the case, then pray this psalm with Jesus as the one being abandoned. Use Psalm 44 as a deep dive into the truth of 2 Corinthians 5:21: "For our sake he made him to be sin who knew no sin, so that in him we might become the righteousness of God."

With every dark phrase of Psalm 44, you can either attack God or revel in the security that is yours. There have been times that I've started praying the psalm in rage against God but soon found myself encountering the work of Christ on my behalf. Other times I have prayed Psalm 44:1–22, and then jumped to Romans 8:37–39. Explore this psalm in prayer, for it is as rich as it is dark.[25]

We belong to God and will never be separated from him. This is why we can praise him, and this is why we can rage.

Chapter 9

Relating to God

Our prayer life is inextricably tied to who it is we are praying to. This first hit home a number of years ago when I decided to preach a sermon series on prayer. I began my preparation in the usual way: I studied the relevant sections of Scripture and reacquainted myself with my favorite books on the subject. Yet something was missing. I had a growing unease about teaching my congregation how to talk to God.

Part of the problem was that my own prayer life was miserable at the time, but pastors regularly teach people to do things they struggle with; it's an occupational hazard. My concerns ran deeper than that. I was nagged by the question: how can I preach on prayer when I haven't first preached on the God we are praying to? That, to me, is where to begin. Just like any relationship, the identity of the person we relate to profoundly affects the nature of the relationship we have with them. For instance, we treat friends differently from spouses, and spouses differently from young children.

Even now, we've talked so much about prayer, but we've yet to consider the astounding fact that God is someone we can, in fact, talk to. How does that even happen? When we speak to God, we make significant assumptions about who he is. We believe he is capable of picking our voices out of the billions of others. It's almost absurd, but we believe the God of the universe sees himself as personally responsible for our lives. Deep and impossible mysteries are called upon each time we talk to God. We pray because we believe that God is a being who listens and comprehends. We pray because we expect that God is relationally accessible.

Or maybe we don't. If you've ever felt that your prayers were bouncing off the ceiling, then you've endured a season where God probably felt inaccessible. Had he seemed near, then your prayers would have shot to heaven like an arrow. For some Christians, this isn't merely a season. Some believers live much of their lives feeling cut off from God. No matter how many books they buy or retreats they attend, prayer is almost impossible because they believe that God is inaccessible. Fix that belief, and prayer will naturally follow.

The God we meet in the Psalter is deeply personal. He is someone who knows and can be known, who loves and can be loved. We can speak openly and honestly with him because he is personally engaged and relationally accessible. The Psalter even goes further, depicting God as one who laughs and fights, who keeps our secrets and gloats over our enemies. God just seems different in the Psalter, and much of that is because he is shown to be most personal in these prayers. It is fitting for us to explore this relatability of God, something we do in this present chapter.

In many ways, this is where we have been heading all along. If this book were a piece of music, I'd want this chapter to be its crescendo. Our journey was never meant to end with the Psalter; the journey ends with God himself. And we can hardly have a book about talking to God without at least one chapter on the God we are talking to. At the same time, I am no theologian and this is no formal study of the doctrine of God.[26] My plan here is to simply describe my experience in hopes that you will grapple with your own notions of God and how you relate to him.

Notions and Inclinations

My first job out of seminary was planting a church in Joplin, Missouri. It is an old frontier town, where the Ozark Mountains give way to the Great Plains. It's blue-collar, agricultural, and pragmatic. After a few months of getting to know the community, we were ready to give a name to the work, one that would reflect both Scripture and that context. I was leaning toward Harvest Presbyterian. I wanted our name to fit nicely into the community instead of whacking it over the head, but then I went to the Joplin mall.

Walking through the mall I saw someone wearing a shirt that read, "Jesus is my homie" and it was like lightning struck. If Joplin was a town that thought of Jesus as a *homie* then it needed to hear something different from us. It needed an exalted Christ, not a buddy. It needed a Jesus who stood over the world in triumph. Joplin needed a King. So, standing between the Cookie Company and the Hallmark Store, I decided on a name for the church: *Christ the King*.

The Jesus I know is not my *homie*. He is Lord and he is God. I take comfort in the picture of Christ from Revelation 1, where his robe is blinding and his voice thunders like a waterfall. I love the Jesus of Revelation 19, where he rides in on a white horse and "treads the winepress of the fury of the wrath of God the Almighty" (v. 15). I don't even know what that phrase means, but I love it. I don't really want a buddy to give me a high five; I want God incarnate who can still the sea. Christ the King is a Christ I can proclaim.

But the story doesn't stop there because relating to God is tricky. I am thankful that God stands *over* my problems, but I am inclined to believe he stands *aloof* from them. I like his authority as King, but I mistakenly transform him into an out-of-touch autocrat. In other words, we are tempted to overcompensate when it comes to the nature of God. The line between God being *incomprehensible* (which he is) and him being *uncomprehended* (which he shouldn't be) is razor thin. It's as thin as the line between God being *present* with his creation (which he is) and him being *indistinguishable* from it (which he shouldn't be). Relating to God means holding difficult concepts in the proper tension, otherwise we'll exaggerate some things about him while neglecting others. We will either end up with God as our *homie* or an absentee ruler.

The Problem with an Inaccessible God

The traditional teaching in Christianity usually highlights how distant God is from us. We definitely don't want God to be our *homie*, so we set him apart through transcendent descriptions and philosophical categories. For instance, see how the Westminster Confession of Faith begins its description of God:

> There is but one only, living, and true God, who is infinite in being and perfection, a most pure spirit, invisible, without body, parts, or passions; immutable, immense, eternal, incomprehensible...[27]

Almost every word in that sentence was chosen to combat our tendency to make God into our own image. God is not like us; he is wholly different. Those same theologians went a step further in their catechism. In keeping with their commitment to the otherness of God, they introduce him with the question: "What is God?"[28] I cringe every time I read their reference to God as a *what*. Could they make him less personal? Westminster's theology has influenced denominations across the Protestant Church and guided Christian spirituality since the seventeenth century. Thinking of God as a *pure-spiritual-what* for hundreds of years must have left a mark on our spiritual practice.

Anytime I think about God being inaccessible, I think of Mount Sinai, particularly the Israelites who stood at its foot. They had a front row seat to the natural distance between humans and God. He descended in "a blazing fire and darkness and gloom and a tempest, and the sound of a trumpet and a voice whose words made the hearers beg that no further messages be spoken to them" (Hebrews 12:18–19). The descriptions make it sound like God was angry with Israel, but this was just God in all his glory. "So terrifying was the sight that Moses said, 'I tremble with fear'" (Hebrews 12:21).

For a while, maybe the sheer spectacle of Sinai held Israel's attention. At some point, however, the distance between them and God took over. They started to believe that God was so *other* that Moses died just for going up the mountain. They speculated that this distance would be the defining mark in their relationship with God, so they gathered their gold and forged it into a golden calf (Exodus 32:1–4). They invented something more accessible. This calf would be something they could relate to. They even revised the story, saying the golden calf sent the plagues, opened the Red Sea, and fed them manna. They couldn't fathom that a God so distant could do anything so personal.

This is a challenge for anyone who believes in God, because he is *wholly other*. The Confession wasn't wrong to describe him that way. But if we stop there, if we think he is nothing but *wholly other*, then we are left with a God that is relationally inaccessible. How do we experience a God whose very presence made Mount Sinai burn like a kiln? If God is a *what*, then how do we even talk to him?

Like the Israelites at the foot of the mountain, we are tempted to change him in order to relate to him. We don't pretend that he is a calf, but we do make out to be our *homie*. We don't have festivals in the name of an idol, but we do sing worship songs that sound like they are for a lost boyfriend. We don't melt down our earrings, but we do plop God on the exam table, dissecting him as if he were nothing more than a combination of doctrines and theological concepts. However we go about it, our flesh wants God to be less than he is.

I've even noticed this habit as it relates to Christian ministry. We talk about the *gospel* as if it were God himself. "The gospel *frees* us to do this," we might say, or "the gospel *enables* us to do that." The gospel, however, is just news that God is freeing and enabling. I think we do this because it's easier to get our minds around the message than it is the person. The gospel has the benefit of being a soundbite. It's the best soundbite in history, but it's a soundbite nonetheless. Ultimately the gospel is just a *what,* containing news about a *who*. It's a channel, not the living water itself.

In my own tradition, we talk more about our standing before God than the God we stand before. Other believers might be more excited about seeing old friends in heaven more than they are God himself. Still others might long for spiritual gifts with more passion than they do the actual Giver of those gifts. We speak of the promises that assure us, the faith that justifies us, the cross that saves us, and the grace that changes us. Is anything missing in all this? Yes! God is. Removing the person of God, we act as if salvation is a consequence of transactions and a collection of benefits.

Grace and faith and heaven are sacred gifts, but they cannot replace our God. That's the real lesson of Sinai: nothing but God can be God. While Israel was down there fiddling with the golden calf, God was on top of the mountain showing Moses how relationally available he truly was. He spoke of personally forgiving his children and he wrote his laws with his own hand. Generation after generation of Israelites would experience the nearness of God. He held their hand in the wilderness and made his home in the middle of their camp. He fought alongside them in Canaan and handpicked their kings.

If that personal God was present at Sinai, how much more is he present with us? We haven't come to Mount Sinai, we've come to Mount Zion. The Scriptures say that we have come to God himself (Hebrews 12:23). There is no need to content ourselves with anything but the person of God. We can have faith in his promises because we know the person who makes them. We can rejoice in the cross because that was our God coming to get us. We can bask in God's grace because it describes the glorious terms of our relationship. The point of our religion is not to enjoy these benefits, but to know our Lord. Our God is *wholly other,* yes, but he is fully capable of relating to his children. Let's discover how.

A Relatable, Accessible God

This God that we've been describing exists as three persons: he is Father and Son and Spirit. These persons help us understand that God is as *relational* as he is *other*. Speaking of the three members of the Trinity, one theologian says that they, "Assume objective relations toward each other, address each other, love each other, and can interact with each other."[29]

In other words, God has a relational capacity within himself. He doesn't need to be changed in order to be experienced. We can address God directly because God is addressable; we can love him because he is already an object of love; and we can interact with him because he has always been interacting. From the beginning, we were fitted for his presence. God made us expecting to relate with us.

Isaiah teaches that God's ear is fully capable of hearing the voice of his children and his arm is fully capable of reaching them, but sin created the separation (Isaiah 59:1–2). God was completely *other* in the garden of Eden, but that wasn't what got in the way. Scripture goes to great lengths to describe just how near God is. Deuteronomy pictures him as a Father who encircles his children and cares for them, who spreads out his wings to catch the strays and guides them to their home (Deuteronomy 32:10–12).

At this point we are so quick to run to Jesus, saying that he is the only reason that God loves us. But that simply isn't the case. According to Scripture, Christ only came because the Father first loved us. We often act as if the Son is shielding us from his Father's sword, but if the Father wanted the sword, then Christ would have come wielding it. God the Father loved us and sent his Son to rescue us. The Son became a human being in order to bring more sons and daughters back to his Father. And now, the Son shares with us the relationship he has always had with his Father. In other words, salvation is a family affair.

Salvation is also an adoption event. God the Father becomes our Father (John 20:17; Romans 8:15; Galatians 4:6; Hebrews 2:10) while God the Son becomes our Brother (John 20:17; Romans 8:29; Hebrews 2:11, 17). Through the Holy Spirit, both Father and Son make their home in the hearts of anyone who believes (John 14:23). We will never be left as orphans. Thinking about our adoption, Cyril of Alexandria wrote, "We are not just baptized into the *name* of the Trinity, we are baptized into the *relations* of the Trinity."[30] From beginning to end, Christian spirituality is a celebration of this access we have to the person of God. It is an access every single psalm expects and claims.

The God of the Psalter

In Psalm 18, David called out to God and the earth rocked and reeled as God came to him, nostrils smoking. Of course the language is poetic, but that's who God is in the Psalter. He is hot-blooded and chasm-crossing. He could never be mistaken for a *what* and is nobody's lost boyfriend. He would never allow himself to be plopped onto some exam table, because the God of the Psalms is an irrepressible *who*.

I discovered this glorious personhood of God by praying one psalm in particular. Psalm 109 charged into my life like a grizzly bear and completely destroyed the sanctimonious box I'd put God in. It's a terribly angry psalm that unleashes a torrent of curses unlike any contained in the rest of Scripture. It's full of little gems like,

> May his children be fatherless
>   and his wife a widow!
> May his children wander about and beg,
>   seeking food far from the ruins they inhabit!
> May the creditor seize all that he has;
>   may strangers plunder the fruits of his toil!
> Let there be none to extend kindness to him,
>   nor any to pity his fatherless children! (vv. 9–12)

Can you imagine praying this? If you pray the Psalms then you will.

This wasn't a God I had ever studied before. This God was a who. In Psalm 109, God is a person who "gets it." He keeps a list of our enemies and goes after our bullies. This was no dispassionate substance from a textbook. This was no distant King who stood aloof in my time of need. This was someone who might toy with pharaoh or make a donkey to talk. This was the kind of person who'd have his people pray that Babylonian children would get dashed on the rocks (Psalm 137:9)! This God was completely terrifying and wholly mesmerizing. I had finally discovered the exhilarating truth of Psalm 56:9: "This I know, that God is for me."

To this day, it surprises me how I met the person of God in Psalm 109. I am one of the least angry people I know, yet I met God in the angriest chapter in the Bible. And I met him there because he made me say those crazy things. God, as I had known him, would never let me talk like that. He would have plugged his ears! There was more to it, though. Praying Psalm 109 showed me that what I lack in anger, I more than make up for in resentment. God coaxed that out of me. He knew I was filthy, and he wanted it to come out—all of it.

Psalm 109 is like the vent valve on a pressure cooker. If God were nothing but an impersonal substance, he wouldn't be willing to pop the valve. He wouldn't understand our innermost feelings and he might not want to hear us scream. But there he is, giving us psalms to get it out of our system, then staying with us to pick up the pieces. We don't need to clean up our thoughts before we come to him. In fact, Psalm 109 teaches us to dirty them up a bit. This was not the God I had conceived of for myself. This was not the God who took a wait and see approach to my life.

Relating to God

Prayer is the chief exercise of faith because our faith is in a person. Like any relationship, ours will grow and change the longer we walk alongside the Lord. Prayer is foremost because the relationship is forged through years of speaking to each other, person-to-person. Our job is to keep believing that God is a willing and active participant in our lives. We need to understand that he is so much more accessible than we ever thought. We need to know that we can truly cultivate an awareness of his personal presence in our lives.

But many of us are settling for less than God himself. Maybe we have used Christian spirituality to create little fortresses for ourselves. We manage personal risk and fortify ourselves against life's worst-case scenario. Maybe we have just been going through the motions or contenting ourselves with the mere benefits of salvation. Psalm 17 describes these lesser desires as having our portion in this life, but the psalmist is having none of it. He will only be satisfied with God himself: "As for me, I shall behold your face in righteousness; when I awake, I shall be satisfied with your likeness" (v. 15).

Our religion is about meeting God. It is the most important meeting in the world. Praying the Psalms has helped me expect to meet God when I open the Bible. We can learn great truths from Scripture, certainly, but praying Scripture allows us to meet him in those pages. Psalmic prayer demands that we lay down our highlighters, set aside our notepads, and start talking to the One who is present in the word. Instead of opening our Bibles to learn some-*thing*, we can open our Bibles to meet some-*One*.

Reflection 9: On Stillness

Praying Psalm 123

Psalmic spirituality is the ancient path to God, and I associate it with peace and stillness. I imagine a lonely trail through the deserts of Palestine. When I think about spirituality that comes from the desert, I often remember the one time I backpacked in the desert. I was overwhelmed by stillness. I ended each day watching the sun dip silently below the western horizon. Then I ate dinner in the lingering twilight. After that, I turned eastward to watch a full moon rise over desert mountains. The peace of that place felt ancient. It was solitary, silent, and still. No wonder so many spiritual seekers found God in the desert.

The problem is we live on divided highways, not ancient paths. We run from one thing to another and are bombarded from every direction. One famous thinker longed for a less distracted age, back when

> People decided what they wanted to read, obtained that work with difficulty, and because it was generally written in such a bland style, they would really have to want to read it in order to find it engaging ... [People consumed information] more sparingly, frugally, and simply ... As a result, time remained for inner reflection, for thought, for mental recalibration ... The mind remained its own master. There was no restless knocking at its door.[31]

This quote comes from a chapter aptly named "Distracted Thinking," written by Abraham Kuyper in 1911. Kuyper believed that daily newspapers, weekly periodicals, and the surge in book publishing caused us to be less focused. If he could only see us now!

Funny coincidence: I am writing this reflection from the tiny waiting room at my doctor's office. We are all squished together, almost shoulder to shoulder. The person across from me plays a game on their phone with the volume blaring, while the person next to him has a conversation on speakerphone. Two people are crunching chips, and another keeps coughing. I wait for my name to be called like I'm waiting for the rapture.

This raises the question: can we cultivate a sense of God's presence in such a noisy place? Can we find him in such a distracted time? How can we experience God amidst the crazy? Peter of Damascus advised monks in the twelfth century that spirituality was best achieved by "living a life without distraction, far from all worldly care, removing ourselves from human society ... Instead, having one concern."[32] That seems laughable.

However, spirituality does require that we unplug from the noise of this world long enough to hear echoes from the other. Christian spirituality begins with corporate worship, but that is probably just once a week. Even our morning Bible study and prayer is forgotten by midday. With that in mind, I suggest we learn to make *stillness* an ongoing spiritual practice. Tiny doses of stillness, sprinkled throughout our day, can remind us of spiritual truths that hide behind the busy world we see.

Thinking back on the Psalms of Ascent, we might remember that Psalm 122 marked the moment when religious pilgrims stepped foot in Jerusalem. They traveled from distant and volatile homelands (Psalm 120), enduring the difficulty of ancient travel (Psalm 121). By Psalm 122, however, they stood within the gates of the holy city. The psalm describes the tangled streets of the city and the sheer mass of humanity that ascended to her. People from every Jewish tribe arrived within days of each other, each heeding the call. Psalm 122 prays for the peace of Jerusalem but that was political peace since Jerusalem buzzed with religious activity.

Then comes Psalm 123. It marks the moment the pilgrim finally entered the temple. But chaos reigned even in this holy place. Jesus described the temple as a religious marketplace and a survey of Leviticus reminds the reader that the temple was an outright slaughterhouse. But you wouldn't know that from the psalm.

> To you I lift up my eyes,
>   O you who are enthroned in the heavens!
> Behold, as the eyes of servants
>   look to the hand of their master,
> as the eyes of a maidservant
>   to the hand of her mistress,
> so our eyes look to the LORD our God,
>   till he has mercy upon us. (vv. 1–2)

The psalmist gazed beyond the deafening noise and nauseating smells to contemplate the God who sat enthroned upon the cherubim. This psalm is the picture of stillness in the midst of chaos.

Psalm 123:2 describes a servant hovering behind his master, watching only his hands. For some reason this always makes me think less about the ancient world and more about a dinner scene from a British TV show. I picture the wait staff coming to and fro among the seated guests, but the master's personal servant only waits for the all-too-familiar pause that tells him it's time to act. He waits for a raised finger that no one else would notice. The servant's whole world is reduced to the smallest gestures of his master's hand. The servant is fixated, controlled by the movement of his master. I'm sure the silverware was clanking, but the servant blocked out the sound. I'm sure there was laughter and gossip, but the servant simply waits.

Peter of Damascus was extreme in his advice, but he wasn't altogether wrong. Rejecting the world allows us to embrace our one true concern. When I watched the moonrise in the desert, there was literally nothing else for me to do. It was stillness by default. For the pilgrim in the temple, stillness had to be achieved, carved out and defended. The psalmist had to learn to still himself because the world wasn't going to be still for him. Finding that stillness allowed him to look upon the person he'd traveled so far to meet.

Psalm 123 has inspired me to practice spiritual stillness. It teaches that we can be near God and contemplate him, no matter where we are. We don't need tranquility to experience stillness because this isn't about worldly calm. If you can find a restful place, great, but the psalmist didn't have that luxury. Psalm 123 is about divine focus. Divine focus is easier when life is calm but it's most needed when life isn't. Here is how I go about it.

I start by asking myself: what is God doing right now?

I've done this long enough that the question alone brings a wave of calm to my heart.

God is at rest. God has no appointments today, he simply is. He isn't trying to catch a bus nor is he catching every stoplight. He doesn't have company coming over tonight, so he doesn't need to buy groceries and clean the house. God doesn't have more family members going in more directions than he has cars to take them.

God possesses all within himself. God is unrattled and unprovoked. Nothing acts upon him, nothing moves him, and he never changes. He needs nothing. God's stillness is baked into who he is as God.

So, back to the question: what is God doing right now?

God is still, and you are his servant.

You don't busy yourself with anything other than your master's work. You focus your attention on your master's hand alone. You aren't listening to the gossip at the table, the clanking of dishes, or the fake laughter from the guests. No, your whole existence is reduced to his tiniest gestures. It controls you like a puppet on a string. But his hand is still.

To quote Paul, your master is not "served by human hands, as though he needed anything" (Acts 17:25). He has everything so he is still. You are controlled by him and so are still, too, sharing his completeness and stillness. He doesn't need you to do anything for him, and it probably feels like he's the only one that doesn't. He simply *is*, so you are too.

Our lives will not slow down, but we can find our master's hand in the chaos. At the grocery store or doing laundry, in a meeting or at a stoplight, we can locate our master's hand and watch its stillness. We can participate in the master's stillness because his movements dictate ours. Even doing this in a passing moment will cultivate your awareness of him and bring you peace.

The assignment in this reflection is to be near God and share in his stillness. It may be easier to learn somewhere calm before taking it into the streets, so find a restful place if you need to.

Begin with the question: what is God doing right now?

Meditate on his work being done.

Look at your master's hand and experience his peace. Let his stillness be your stillness. Let his rest be the source of your calm. Let it relax your muscles. One of God's gifts to us is his stillness. He is at rest and invites us to enter that rest alongside him (Hebrews 4:1–11). It is a redemptive rest, but there is no reason it can't affect our blood pressure and stress levels.

When my wife gives me a list of things to do, I feel a wave of tension. Likewise, I feel relaxed if she tells me the work is done. Is God less of a person? Is he less real? Can't his finished work affect our mood and body? This isn't about controlling your breathing or something mystical, this is simply the act of paying attention to God the person. We don't *pretend* that he is near, we *believe* that he is. We experience his presence like we would any other person. And God is glad that you have chosen the good: sitting and listening (Luke 10:38–42).

Our hearts can step away from the noise even when our bodies are surrounded by it. We can be near him wherever we are. This is what the psalmist had to do. He teaches us in the psalm what Peter of Damascus had to teach those monks: *remove distractions and have one concern.*

Stillness means *being*, without having to *do*. It means *waiting* without *wanting*.[33] It is like a servant watching the hand of his contented master.

I will close with a delightful story from one of my favorite books on prayer that inspires me to simply be near God:

> St. John Vianney, a nineteenth-century priest in rural France, noticed a farmer who would come into the church every morning and evening and just sit there with no Bible, no prayer book, no rosary. Finally, the saint asked the farmer what he was doing. "I look at him," the farmer replied, "and he looks at me; and we are happy."[34]

Chapter 10

Meeting God

In 701 BC the Assyrian army advanced on the cities of Judah. They were the most powerful nation in that part of the world, having already swept through much of the region. They had even conquered the northern tribes of Israel twenty years prior, leaving Judah to fend for herself. As part of their military offensive, Assyria mounted a devastating campaign of psychological warfare. Their messenger claimed that Yahweh had abandoned Judah, but even if Yahweh did fight for them it would make no difference. Assyria was so powerful that no god delivered any of its people from their hand. If the gods of Hamath and Arpad were powerless to save, so too was Yahweh.[35]

That was the message laid before Judah's king, Hezekiah. Meanwhile, God sent a message of his own. Through the prophet Isaiah, God told Hezekiah what he almost always told his people: fear not. Hezekiah now found himself in an age-old dilemma. He had two competing narratives. Isaiah's message said, "I am God," and Assyria's message said, "No he's not." This was basically the dilemma Eve faced all the way back in the garden of Eden, and it's the same thing we've been wrestling with ever since. Hezekiah had to decide if he would succumb to earthly power or resist it by faith. Would he entrust his nation to the hand of Assyria or the hand of God?

In one of the better religious moments in the Old Testament, Hezekiah took his fear and confusion to the Lord. We could forgive Hezekiah for doing a quick inventory of his military assets, but he went to the temple instead. Maybe he recited Psalm 33 as he made his way to the temple:

> The king is not saved by his great army;
>   a warrior is not delivered by his great strength.
> The war horse is a false hope for salvation,
>   and by its great might it cannot rescue. (vv. 16–17)

There were no military assets that could tip the scales. Hezekiah and his people were in over their heads and that's where religion does its best work. Once in the temple, Hezekiah spread out the Assyrian's letter before the Lord. Looking at the letter and looking up towards the throne of God, Hezekiah prayed:

> "O Lord of hosts, God of Israel, enthroned above the cherubim, you are the God, you alone, of all the kingdoms of the earth; you have made heaven and earth. Incline your ear, O Lord, and hear; open your eyes, O Lord, and see; and hear all the words of Sennacherib, which he has sent to mock the living God. Truly, O Lord, the kings of Assyria have laid

> waste all the nations and their lands, and have cast their gods into the fire. For they were no gods, but the work of men's hands, wood and stone. Therefore they were destroyed. So now, O Lord our God, save us from his hand, that all the kingdoms of the earth may know that you alone are the Lord." (Isaiah 37:15–20)

This scene is compelling because it's so real. We can imagine Hezekiah calling to his attendants to be left alone with God. We can almost feel the cold stone floor and picture the candlelight. We can imagine the smells, the echoes, and the stillness of the temple. I think about this moment often because I almost envy having a physical place to go like the temple. Yet what stands out most is Hezekiah's honesty. It's naive, but it's the childlike heart of prayer. There, on the floor of the temple, Hezekiah asks the Lord, "Have you seen this letter?"

With that simple question Hezekiah forgoes his position as *ruler* and takes his rightful place as *ruled*. God created us to receive his judgments not to judge things for ourselves. Imagine if Eve had done the same as Hezekiah. Think how different things would be if she simply asked God, "Have you heard what this serpent is saying?" We were never meant to *judge*; we were only meant to *ask*. This kind of dependence is worship in its simplest form because it acknowledges the authority of God in the most basic way possible. Hezekiah wasn't worshiping because he was in the temple; he was worshiping because his soul was bowed before the rightful King.

I like to think that this fateful meeting in the sanctuary was the inspiration for Psalm 73, and we will use that psalm and Hezekiah's experience to investigate our final topic in this book.[36] Psalm 73 is the proper end for a book such as this because it stands like a giant within the Psalter. It is the perfect example of the transformative nature of worship. Throughout this book, we have described the various features of psalmic prayer, exploring how to meet God, and even the God that we meet. But in this last chapter, we will celebrate the power of that meeting. Let's follow this psalm as it leads us into the presence of our Lord.

Futility in the World

The presence of God is a place of nourishment and delight, but neither the psalmist nor Hezekiah was living in such a place. The first half of Psalm 73 describes a world in rebellion. It's a place where the wicked have it easy. They never suffer and they live in luxury until the day they die. "They are not stricken like the rest of mankind" (Psalm 73:5). Pride, violence, and malice fill their hearts as they are free to scoff, threaten, and strut. One of the most frustrating things for the psalmist is how no one calls their wickedness to account. They flaunt themselves before the world and God, and neither do anything about it: "[The wicked] say, 'How can God know? Is there knowledge in the Most High?' " (v. 11)

The Psalms are quick to wonder if God is paying attention to the struggles of his saints, and Psalm 73 is no exception. If sin makes life fun and easy, then why be good? If God isn't going to call wickedness to account, then why are we working so hard to be righteous? It is a thread of frustration that weaves its way throughout the Psalter and gnaws at the heart of our psalmist.

To put it in Hezekiah's context, why did Assyria's king get to mock God and dominate nation after nation? God said he would judge such wickedness, but Assyria just kept getting stronger. Meanwhile, it was like God wanted his own people as weak as possible. God didn't want Judah to amass wealth or fortify themselves with powerful armies. God wanted his people to be a kingdom of priests. But the world didn't belong to priests, it belonged to the Assyrians. Just like in our world today, power belongs to the powerful. Egypt and Assyria were both heavyweights in the region and already at war. If Judah could just align with Egypt, then they might find shelter, yet God would hunt them down and accuse them of sin.

It doesn't seem fair that God would care so little about Assyria's wrongs and so much about Judah's. This is the general accusation of Psalm 44:20–21. Why does the Lord remain silent while his people are chased and beaten, but he always seems to notice when they fall into sin? In other words, Hezekiah had to remain faithful and wait on God, and if he acted like Assyria's king, then God would take away his throne. It didn't make sense. In Psalm 73, such futility starts to boil:

> All in vain have I kept my heart clean
> and washed my hands in innocence.
> For all the day long I have been stricken
> And rebuked every morning. (vv. 13–14)

The first half of Psalm 73 is a rant about the injustice of God. It's filled with frustration and resentment. As we have seen, prayer is the place to voice such thoughts; we can say anything, believe anything, and swing at God with all we have. But the psalmist acts differently outside of prayer, or maybe he acts differently *because* he prayed. His was in a leadership position, and his faith crisis had to be a private one. He walked the walk of faith even when his heart was melting: "If I had said, 'I will speak thus,' I would have betrayed the generation of your children" (v. 15).

This is the position that every faith-leader finds themselves in, whether Old Testament king or twenty-first century pastor. Believe when no one else believes. Pastors see the same evidence that causes our people to panic, and our hearts are hardly stronger than anyone else's, but we believe nonetheless. We have to believe God will make a way when it looks like no way exists; that God will heal, that the power of sin can be broken, that evil will fail, that someone will be delivered, or that Christ is still on his throne. It doesn't matter if the church is burning to the ground, we believe and so we speak (2 Corinthians 4:13). I once heard a preacher say something that has stuck with me throughout my ministry: pastors have to out-believe their congregation.[37]

The Wearisome Task

The world is broken. Nations rage and wickedness struts about the earth. There is injustice and oppression, illness and death, yet God doesn't seem to make things right. In fact, he's harder on us than he is on anyone else. Meanwhile, we have to keep believing when evidence points to the contrary and sin is far more enticing. This is what bothers the psalmist and possibly Hezekiah; it certainly bothers us. In a world with such futility and frustration, it never surprises me when a believer has a crisis of faith, it only surprises me that believers don't have them more often.

Adding to the confusion is the fact that we live in a fog of distortion. Our minds are as broken as our hearts. We were designed to experience life as it is filtered by God, to receive his interpretation of reality. We were created to be like an antenna, receiving our signals from the Lord. But sin has broken that antenna. We don't process the world correctly or, more to the point, we often process the world as if we are on our own. The psalmist admits that his doubts were steeped in this fog of sinful distortion. They led him down a dark path full of frustration and resentment. He confesses:

> When my soul was embittered,
> 	when I was pricked in heart,
> I was brutish and ignorant;
> 	I was like a beast toward you. (Psalm 73: 21–22)

Of course the psalmist was bitter. Feeling alone brings out the worst in us. God created us to ask, to listen, and to receive. Anyone who looks within themselves finds nothing but an empty space and experiences only turmoil. Like the psalmist, Isaiah describes this lonely experience:

Let him who walks in darkness
and has no light
trust in the name of the LORD
and rely on his God.
Behold, all you who kindle a fire,
who equip yourselves with burning torches!
Walk by the light of your fire,
and by the torches that you have kindled!
This you have from my hand:
you shall lie down in torment. (Isaiah 50:10b–11)

Torment is a great word to describe the first half of Psalm 73. We weren't designed to walk by the light of our own fire or take counsel in our own soul. Left to ourselves, we exaggerate certain things and minimize others; we find false hope with one breath and catastrophize with the next. It is a wearisome task indeed.

When Eve thought she had to judge for herself she listened to the serpent. Abraham thought he had to fulfill the promise himself, so he slept with Hagar. Elijah thought he was alone, so he fled from Jezebel. When we think it is up to us, we wilt. Compare that to Joseph, who endured numerous trials because he kept expecting God to show up. Or Caleb, who heard the report about giants in the promised land and just assumed God would do gigantic things. One person was not stronger, more optimistic, or more holy than another. What moved the needle in one direction over the other was the belief that God is present.

That is why the psalmist went to the sanctuary of God, because the wearisome task was too much. I imagine Hezekiah in much the same place, gripped by the fear of an enemy, simmering in frustration at God, and pressured by the nature of his position. It would be enough to swallow anyone. At times like this only the Lord himself can be our consolation.

> But when I thought how to understand this,
>   it seemed to me a wearisome task,
> until I went into the sanctuary of God;
>   then I discerned their end. (Psalm 73:16–17)

The Sanctuary of God

It's tempting to think that prayer is just about clearing our heads or verbally processing our problems. Hezekiah faced a tremendous task and the simple act of talking may have unburdened his mind. Certainly talking through our problems can help, but that's not really why we pray. Prayer is a meeting. It is a person-to-person interaction. Like the sanctuary itself, the Psalter is like a conference room where a meeting between God and man takes place.

In that meeting, Hezekiah took his proper place as a creature dependent upon his Creator. Hezekiah wasn't just going to the temple that day, he went to the Rock that was higher than him. He fled and he hid. He assessed himself, assessed his God, and he chose to take refuge. In so doing, he experienced the world as it truly is. Through worshiping God, he placed God on his throne. God had always been there, of course, but it isn't always the case in our hearts. We have to actively enthrone God with our praise, or we will invent something else to take his place (Psalm 22:3).[38]

Interestingly, though, nothing physical changed because Hezekiah met God. It wasn't as if he emerged from the sanctuary with a flaming sword, and it wasn't a Psalm 18 moment where he called on the Lord and the earth rocked and reeled. Deliverance through worship is often more subtle than that. In fact, the enemies were as strong and proud after he worshiped as they were before! It wasn't his enemies who were destroyed, it was the deception.

The view from the presence of God is clear and true. From there, Hezekiah saw that these world powers were mere shadows before the Lord (Psalm 73:20). The enemies appeared immovable, but their feet actually stood on slippery places (Psalm 73:18). They wouldn't last. Only God would remain. Psalm 9 has a line that I love: "Let the nations know that they are but men!" In Psalm 73, God didn't remind the nations that they are merely men, but he did remind the psalmist, and that might be more important.

Fleeing to the temple allowed Hezekiah the chance to experience being God's treasured possession. He entered into personal communion with God, and God nurtured him because of it. This is quite different from going off to study Isaiah's message. Hezekiah could have hired linguists and hand-writing experts to break down the words of God, but he spoke to God directly instead. This meeting gave Hezekiah the chance to do something he couldn't do in mere study. Hezekiah could look to the heavens and ask of God: "Say to my soul, 'I am your salvation!'" (Psalm 35:3).

The importance of this worship experience can't be overstated. God provided Hezekiah with a prophet, a message, and a plan for deliverance. Hezekiah was mostly sidelined for the whole thing! Even God's promise to save Judah was "for the sake of my servant David" (Isaiah 37:35). That's the hard truth about God's grace: it often takes us out of the picture at the very moment we want to be at the center. Would Hezekiah have a sneaky thought that God really only loved David? Would he imagine God as merely keeping his promise and checking this off the list? Anyone that lives by God's grace has to wrestle with this question, even Christians. Is our salvation just an eventuality based on previous things like Jesus and the cross?

Hezekiah found his answer in the sanctuary. We all do. God didn't rebuke Hezekiah for needing a dose of reassurance after hearing Isaiah's message, and he didn't strike him down for entering the temple unannounced. Then there's the Assyrian letter. Like a child, Hezekiah actually spread out the letter before the Lord. I wonder what God thought as he watched Hezekiah fumble awkwardly with the pages. God had already dealt with this, hadn't he? God certainly didn't need to see the letter itself. He knew what that letter would say before pen was ever put to parchment. Yet God waited for Hezekiah to finish unrolling it. He listened as Hezekiah read through it. God did this because what he wanted most was Hezekiah's heart.

I don't know all that God spoke to Hezekiah's heart that day, but it probably went something like this:

> Even to your old age I am he,
>   and to gray hairs I will carry you.
> I have made, and I will bear;
>   I will carry and will save. (Isaiah 46:4)

One of the greatest lessons from the psalmist's crisis is how much the Father loves his children. God welcomed Hezekiah into his sanctuary. God was glad to see Hezekiah because God always likes to talk to his children. God wasn't just mechanically keeping a promise to David, he took an active and personal interest in the weight that burdened the soul of his child. That, more than anything, is why we pray.

The Lord actually did see the letter that Hezekiah spread before him and got as angry as Hezekiah had hoped. God fought for Judah's king and kept his people safe. The angel of the Lord eventually killed 185,000 warriors and the king of Assyria was soon killed by his own son. But the victories did not continue. Ultimately, it was Babylon running through the streets of Jerusalem and swinging axes in the temple. It raises the question of whether the whole Hezekiah-temple event was worth it. Did God allow Assyria to fail just so Babylon could succeed? Asked another way, did going to the sanctuary *work*?

Psalm 73 answers this question. The goal was never about changing the king's perspective or even winning a battle. The goal was

God himself. God was the prize. The king met God in the temple that day, and the meeting itself was the most important thing in all the world. Psalm 73 ends with some of the most powerful lines in all the Psalter because it reminds us that it was always, only, about meeting God. The Psalm closes with the prayer that we used at the beginning of this book:

> Nevertheless, I am continually with you;
>   you hold my right hand.
> You guide me with your counsel,
>   and afterward you will receive me to glory.
> Whom have I in heaven but you?
>   And there is nothing on earth that I desire besides you.
> My flesh and my heart may fail,
>   but God is the strength of my heart and my portion
>   forever.
> For behold, those who are far from you shall perish;
>   you put an end to everyone who is unfaithful to you.
> But for me it is good to be near God;
>   I have made the Lord GOD my refuge,
>   that I may tell of all your works. (Psalm 73:23–28)

Reflection 10: The Path Forward

It would be appropriate to use this final reflection as an encouragement to pray the Psalms, but hopefully you have already begun your psalmic journey and don't need a rousing send-off from me. Instead,

I would like to consider spiritual practice in general, and what comes next for those who pray the Psalms. I specifically want to address other believers, like myself, who struggle with spiritual wanderlust.

For much of my life, I have been on a quest to resolve a spiritual unrest within my soul. In my mid-twenties I flirted with the idea of joining a Catholic monastery and have always loved Eastern Orthodox spirituality. It's been easy to think my spiritual home was wherever I wasn't, or that "my people" weren't at whatever church I attended. I was always looking for something, but I wasn't even sure what. Mostly, I just believed that the spiritual grass was greener in other pastures. When I was young and free, I grabbed at any and every spiritual adventure. Once I had family and life commitments, this wanderlust was relegated to the confines of my heart.

Spirituality should bring stability, but for many of us it is associated with restlessness. My friends and I have dealt with this for long enough that I actually saw the spiritual vagabond as the intended audience for this book. I think there is a sizable group of believers who want more than what mere church and small groups provide. We want to be more than good Christians; we want our lives to be touched by God. Perhaps you are that person and you arrived at this book as part of your restless journey. Maybe you are hoping that psalmic prayer will be the practice that finally brings rest to your soul. If that's the case, I am honored that my book could be part of your story.

When I first discovered psalmic prayer, I thought my fruitless search was over. I felt a little bit like Josiah when he discovered

God's law (2 Kings 22). Recovering the ancient practice ignited a mini-revival in my heart. For some reason, I found it easier to schedule time to pray psalms than to pray my own words, which meant that my prayers didn't just get better, they became more frequent. I was almost giddy about finally having a prayer life. At last, I could draw from my own spiritual experience to help others with practical, spiritual direction. The joy lasted for a couple of years as I prayed the Psalms almost every day.

At some point, however, things began to change. As I got to know the Psalter better, its prayers lost the sense of surprise they once had. I was less stretched by them and less excited. That practice which first revolutionized my spiritual life was no longer revolutionary. I prayed the Psalms less and less until I quit them altogether. It wasn't a crisis of faith as much as I was just moving on. I assumed that psalmic prayer had given me all that it could.

But when I finally stopped, I struggled to replace the real-ness of praying Scripture. I missed the surety of it more than anything. So, after a few months of barely praying, I embarked on a quest to find my next experience. I went shopping for some incense. I bought frankincense because it seemed more biblical than the incense we used at home. I sat on the floor of my office, lit the incense, and prayed while watching the smoke rise. I felt spiritually alive for the first time in months. I felt like my prayers were real again, and that God was hearing them. And then I thought, *What am I doing?*

Incense may be biblical, but I wasn't using it biblically. In fact, I'm embarrassed to admit that story because it makes me sound like a spiritual junkie. But that's precisely why I share it. Sitting there watching the smoke, I realized that I found more joy in spiritual discovery than I find in the presence of God. I have always been fixated on the search for God, even at the expense of God himself. This fixation means there is an ever-increasing pile of spiritual practices that I once used but eventually discarded. But perhaps those practices only quit working because they quit being new.

I believe this search for the new is an epidemic in modern spirituality. It's a reason that we switch small groups, worship styles, churches, and denominations. On a private level, it is why we try a devotional, then jump to podcasts, then find a spiritual director, then shut out everything for an inductive Bible study. Change can be good, and we sometimes need it, but are we changing too many things, too often, and for the wrong reasons? Are we looking for something new only to realize that something new is *all* we are looking for? If so, then we have a problem.

Psalmic prayer will eventually become ordinary. When it does, you will have to decide whether you want to *find* something different or if you want to *be* someone different. That moment happened for me with the incense. It's ironic that such a silly attempt at spirituality brought one of my biggest spiritual epiphanies. I realized in that moment that I wanted off that ride I'd spent so much of my life on. I wanted to quit looking for my spiritual home and start making my home in the Psalter. So I went back to praying the Psalms and shut out all the enticing alternatives. I've realized that there are no greener pastures. In short, I decided to limit myself and my spirituality.

The great fathers and mothers of our faith didn't get to where they were by chasing every spiritual practice. In fact, most of them are revered for their willingness to live with less. Less food, less money, less comfort, less pleasure. The saints were chaste, not chasing. Whether they were great preachers or quiet servants, the names we know are the names of those who stayed the course.

Thinking back to the desert monks, I imagine that some of them had an unhealthy relationship to the flamboyant nature of their spiritual experience. Yet I admire them for not flip-flopping on how to know God. They didn't spend a year with their favorite teacher, then three months in the desert, then six months on a pilgrimage, then two years doing ministry. No, they limited themselves to find God in the simplest way. They practiced their simple spirituality every hour of every day, sometimes for half their lives. Even the craziest of them were shockingly routine in their pursuit of God. Their amazing experiences were a product of growth and perseverance, not the result of finding the next amazing practice.

My heart goes out to anyone that struggles with this. People like us have to learn the hard lessons of self-discipline and commitment. We have to learn the ascetic practice of telling ourselves *no* when our itchy hearts cry *yes*. These are not pleasant lessons to learn. It means quitting the "spiritual journey" and making yourself at home. It means befriending your discontent instead of always trying to resolve it. It means realizing that your restless heart is just eternity etched on your soul and there will be no earthly fix. It means accepting the ordinary, but only because our God is God of the ordinary. Our Lord loves us too much to give us a spiritual practice that could supply all the things he himself wants to give us.

All that being said, the Psalter is an invaluable companion in your soul's quest for God. Only after praying the Psalms for a long period of time do you finally experience its brightest treasures.

Praying the Psalms will teach you Scripture without you even noticing. God intended the Psalter to be a mini-Bible and it truly works that way. Over the years, you'll discover how much of the New Testament sits on a psalmic foundation. You will catch Paul's dependence on psalmic ideas that even the best commentaries miss. Praying the Psalms means living within the book that provides deep structure to the entire New Testament. It is a fascinating experience.

I still struggle to pray the Psalms every day. There are stretches where I get away from the practice, sometimes for months. When I return to them, however, I feel like I'm walking into a home that God and I have shared. We've had some great and some challenging times inside the Psalter. I'm reminded of those times when I pray the Psalms, as if his and my history are woven together in psalmic words. Which is probably how it should be.

Spirituality is a long journey that requires faith and patience. It is an ancient path that must be walked over and over again. Sometimes it will be a delight and sometimes it will be so ordinary you'll think nothing supernatural is happening. In other words, Daniel's angels probably won't show up to reassure you that you are loved and that you are being heard. But you keep walking that ancient path nonetheless.

In each of these reflections I have offered an assignment to direct you as you pray the Psalms. The assignment in this final reflection is just to keep praying the Psalms after their glory fades. Pray through all one hundred and fifty psalms, whether that takes a month or a year, and then do it again and again. I encourage you not to discard this practice when it stops feeling revolutionary. Make it past the exciting moments and come to know these prayers as you would an old and dependable friend. You will still be surprised by them, just in different ways. You will still find nourishment, just at different depths.

The goal of this book has been to help you meet God. That meeting is more often the result of endurance than it is discovery and surprise. So be of good courage and keep walking that ancient path. Follow it, knowing exactly where it is leading you:

> You make known to me the path of life;
> in your presence there is fullness of joy;
> at your right hand are pleasures forevermore.
>
> (Psalm 16:11)

Acknowledgments

I have dedicated this book to my wife and daughters because without them, there would be no book. My wife's honesty is my compass, and her love is my security. Her faith teaches me, and her prayers uphold me. Thank you Lee Ann. Thank you for insisting that I write this book, and for reading (not to mention grading!) so many drafts. Thank you to my daughters: Jennalee, Adeline, and Tarikwa. Your pride in me is my greatest accomplishment, and your friendship is my greatest treasure. The vigor with which you three pursue life inspires me to do more with my own. You are my peace, love, and joy this side of heaven.

Thank you, also, to the rest of my family. To my dad, Don Dunn: thank you for showing me what it means to follow the Lord, love my family, and lead the church. To my mom, Cathy Dunn: thank you for sharing with me your love of knowledge and for all those long talks about philosophy and life. To my sister, Shannon Lowe: thank you for being my oldest friend and fellow seeker, and thank you for helping me fall in love with the English language.

This being my first book, there is not enough space to thank all of my friends and mentors who deserve to be mentioned. However, I feel compelled to name Chris Miller and Ted Wenger, as I might not still be in ministry without your care and guidance. Thank you to all those who walked alongside me, taught me, and encouraged me to write. Most notably, I would like to thank Bobby and Marty File who stand as towering figures in my faith journey.

I would like to thank the monks at Our Lady of Clear Creek Abbey. Your hospitality provided me the space to first explore the practices detailed in this book. Thank you to my dear friend Kevin Hale, who processed every single aspect of this book with me and who, as always, answered my Hebrew questions. Thank you to all those who have provided their advice, critique, and support: Hunter Bailey, Todd Brewer, Cody Chapman, Lane Tipton, and Thomas Ufer. Any faults in this work are my own, but there would have been more without these friends. Thank you to Dan Scott for tirelessly helping me say more with less. Thank you to my editor, Rachel Welcher, who endured my angst and gave me courage to leave some of my "darlings" on the cutting room floor. Thank you to Lexham Press for believing in this project.

Lastly, I'd like to thank the churches that have played such a big role in my life. First is the congregation of Christ the King Presbyterian Church in Joplin, Missouri. I discovered this practice alongside you, and I hope that you find this finished product a celebration of our work together. Second, I want to thank the congregation of Redeemer Hudson in Union City, New Jersey. Thank you for sharing in this project with me. You read drafts, joined me in study, and followed me in prayer. Through you, as Psalm 107 says, the Lord has satisfied my family's longing soul and through you we have found a city to dwell in.

Works Cited

Athanasius of Alexandria, *Letter to Marcellinus on the Psalms*. Translated by Joel C. Elowsky. ICCS Press, 2017.

Bonhoeffer, Dietrich. *Psalms: The Prayer Book of the Bible*. Augsburg Fortress, 1970.

Chrysostom, John. "The Divine Liturgy." In *Service Books of the Orthodox Church*. St. Tikhon's Seminary Press, 1984.

Chryssavgis, John. "Solitude, Silence, and Stillness: Light from the Palestinian Desert." In *The Philokalia: A Classic Text of Orthodox Spirituality*. Edited by Brock Bingaman and Bradley Nassif. Oxford University Press, 2012.

Elder Thaddeus of Vitovnica. *Our Thoughts Determine Our Lives*. Translated by Ana Smiljanic and Compiled by St. Herman of Alaska Brotherhood. St. Herman of Alaska Brotherhood, 2012.

The ESV Study Bible: English Standard Version. Crossway Bibles, 2008.

Fairbairn, Donald. *Life in the Trinity*. InterVarsity Press, 2009.

Ignatius of Antioch, *The Letters*. Translated by Alistair Stewart. St. Vladimir's Seminary Press, 2013.

Keating, Daniel A. *Appropriation of the Divine Life*. Oxford University Press, 2004.

Keller, Timothy. *The Freedom of Self-Forgetfulness*. 10Publishing, 2012.

Kidner, Derek. *Psalms 1–72*. InterVarsity Press, 1973.

Kuyper, Abraham. *Pro Rege*. Translated by Albert Gootjes. Edited by John Kok with Nelson D. Kloosterman. 3 vols. Lexham Press, 2016.

Letham, Robert. *The Holy Trinity: In Scripture, History, Theology, and Worship*. P&R Publishing, 2004.

Letrende, L. Joseph. When You Pray: A Practical Guide to an Orthodox Life of Prayer. Ancient Faith Publishing, 2017.

Lloyd-Jones, D. Martyn. *Spiritual Depression*. Eerdmans Publishing, 1965.

Luther, Martin. Preface to the Psalter Published at Neuburg on the Danube (1545). In *Luther's Commentary on the First Twenty-Two Psalms*, translated by John Nicolaus Lenker. Sunbury, PA: Lutherans in All Lands, 1903.

Lusk, Herb. 2006. "Commencement Speech at Westminster Seminary."

Murray, John. *Collected Writings*. Vol. 2 of *Select Lectures in Systematic Theology*. Banner of Truth Trust, 1977 (2001).

Old Man Luedecke. 2012. "Jonah and the Whale." Track #2 on *Tender is the Night*. True North Records.

Peter of Damascus. "Seven Forms of Bodily Discipline." In *The Philokalia*. Vol 3. Translated and edited by G. E. H Palmer, Philip Sherrard, Kallistos Ware. Faber and Faber, 1984.

Peterson, Eugene. *A Long Obedience in the Same Direction*. InterVarsity Press, 1980.

Schauss, Hayyim, *The Jewish Festivals*. Translated by Samuel Faffe. Schocken Books, 1938.

Sheehan, Donald. *The Shield of Psalmic Prayer.* Edited by Xenia Sheehan. Ancient Faith Publishing, 2020.

Vos, Geerhardus. *Reformed Dogmatics.* Vol. 1 of *Theology Proper*. Lexham Press, 2012–2014.

Westminster Confession of Faith and Catechisms. The Committee on Christian Education of the Orthodox Presbyterian Church, 2005 (2015).

Westminster Confession of Faith in Modern English. The Evangelical Presbyterian Church, 2010.

Wenham, Gordon. *The Psalter Reclaimed.* Crossway, 2013.

Notes

1 Athanasius, "Letter to Marcellinus on the Interpretation of the Psalms," in *The Life of Anthony*, edited by Emilie Griffin, translated by Robert C. Gregg (Harper San Francisco, 1980), 83–116.

2 Dietrich Bonhoeffer, *Psalms: The Prayer Book of the Bible* (Augsburg Fortress, 1970), 16. Bonhoeffer notes that the Lord's Prayer is a summary of the prayers of Scripture. Each petition in the Lord's Prayer can be traced back to a different theme in the Psalter. As I have become more fluent in psalmic ideas, I hear the echoes of psalms every time I recite the Lord's Prayer. It is amazing, not to mention gracious, to think of Jesus giving us a prayer that covers so much spiritual territory yet is still simple enough for a child to memorize and use.

3 The Psalms that don't address God or lead others to do so, do the following: provide wisdom (1, 49, 127, 133), recount history (78, 105, 106), or praise something other than God (the king in 45 and Zion in 87).

4 Derek Kidner argues that this ancient annotation reveals that "Prayers" may have been the earliest term used for the collection of psalms. Derek Kidner, *Psalms 1–72* (InterVarsity Press, 1973 [2008]), 277.

5 The Psalms have no interest in rhyme or meter because Hebrew poetry used different literary conventions. Repetition and parallelism are the hallmarks of psalmic poetry. One line states a situation, and the following lines intensify it. See, for example, the repetition in Psalm 18:4–5.

6 Didache 8. With both prayer and fasting there is advice on not being like the hypocrites, which is most likely a reference to Jews. In regard

to prayer, the Jews prayed the *Shema* (Deuteronomy 6:4) three times a day and this replacement would parallel the overt replacement offered on days of fasting.

7 Ignatius of Antioch, "Letter to Magnesians," in *The Letters*, trans. Alistair Stewart (St. Vladimir's Seminary Press, 2013), chapter 9.

8 Martin Luther, Preface to the Psalter Published at Neuburg on the Danube (1545), *Luther's Commentary on the First Twenty-Two Psalms*, trans. John Nicolaus Lenker (Sunbury, PA: Lutherans in All Lands, 1903), 14–15.

9 Gordon Wenham, *The Psalter Reclaimed* (Crossway, 2013), 38.

10 I am relying on John Murray's hugely helpful description of progressive sanctification. His treatment appears in his *Collected Writings* (Vol 2, Ch 23) but discussions of it can be found online.

11 See page 136 for discussion of intercessory prayer and the psalter.

12 Elder Thaddeus of Vitovnica, *Our Thoughts Determine Our Lives*, trans. Ana Smiljanic, ed. St. Herman of Alaska Brotherhood (St. Herman of Alaska Brotherhood, 2012), 124.

13 L. Joseph Letrende, *When You Pray: A Practical Guide to an Orthodox Life of Prayer* (Ancient Faith Publishing, 2017), 29.

14 Psalm 34 (and other Davidic psalms) were either written by David or written by others to commemorate David's experience. The Hebrew phrase that introduces these psalms ("of David") could mean either. I will speak as if he is the author, but our point doesn't change if the Psalms were written by someone else.

15 Psalm 77:9 references God's anger shutting up his compassion, so the people were probably enduring some consequence for sin. It may or may not be a reference to the same judgment of Psalm 74.

16 This whole chapter is dealing with this topic from a psalmic/experiential perspective, but I highly recommend Tim Keller's short book entitled

The Freedom of Self-Forgetfulness. It looks at it more from a Pauline/theological perspective.

17 Donald Sheehan, *The Shield of Psalmic Prayer*, ed. Xenia Sheehan (Ancient Faith Publishing, 2020), 15.

18 Eugene Peterson, in his book *A Long Obedience in the Same Direction*, discusses the idea of using a spiritual thermometer to take our own spiritual temperature. I have taken it in my own direction but am indebted to him for introducing the imagery. Eugene Peterson, *A Long Obedience in the Same Direction*, (InterVarsity Press, 1980 [2021]), 38, 78.

19 John Chrysostom, "The Divine Liturgy," in *Service Books of the Orthodox Church*, (St. Tikhon's Seminary Press, 1984 [2010]), 73.

20 *Westminster Confession of Faith in Modern English*, (The Evangelical Presbyterian Church, 2010), chapter 18, section 4.

21 I highly recommend Martyn Lloyd-Jones' book *Spiritual Depression* for anyone who is struggling.

22 Hayyim Schauss, *The Jewish Festivals*, trans. Samuel Faffe (Schocken Books, 1938), 181.

23 See also 42:11 and 43:5.

24 Old Man Luedecke, "Jonah and the Whale," on *Tender is the Night*, True North Records, 2012.

25 Psalm 89 has a similar structure and theme. In some ways it is even more clearly Christological because it roots the goodness of God in the Davidic Promise of 2 Samuel 7, which has profound implications on the life and ministry of Christ.

26 For further reading I recommend *The Holy Trinity* (Letham) and *Life in the Trinity* (Fairbairn).

27 *Westminster Confession of Faith*, Chapter 2, Section 1.

28 *Westminster Larger Catechism,* Question 7.

29 Geerhardus Vos, *Reformed Dogmatics,* vol. 1 of *Theology Proper* (Lexham Press, 2012–2014), 43, question 12c.

30 Daniel A Keating, *Appropriation of the Divine Life* (Oxford University Press, 2004), 56; emphasis added.

31 Abraham Kuyper, *Pro Rege, vol. 1,* trans. Albert Gootjes, ed. John Kok with Nelson D. Kloosterman (Lexham Press, 2016), 61.

32 John Chryssavgis, "Solitude, Silence, and Stillness: Light from the Palestinian Desert," in *The Philokalia: A Classic Text of Orthodox Spirituality*, vol. 3, ed. Brock Bingaman and Bradley Nassif (Oxford University Press, 2012), 89.

33 Bingaman and Nassif, *The Philokalia,* 269.

34 Letendre, *When You Pray*, 9.

35 This story is recounted in both 2 Kings 19 and Isaiah 37.

36 Throughout this chapter I will act as if Psalm 73 was Hezekiah's experience even though I don't know if that is actually the case. Their situations are similar, but delineating between the psalmist and Hezekiah would get difficult to read.

37 Herb Lusk, commencement address at Westminster Theological Seminary, 2006.

38 The Psalter is willing to speak experientially about this enthronement, and we can too.

ALSO AVAILABLE FROM LEXHAM PRESS

Reading the Psalms as Scripture

Visit lexhampress.com to learn more